Preparing Youths
for the Workplace

Preparing Youths for the Workplace

Editors

Jessie Ee
Agnes Chang

World Scientific

NEW JERSEY · LONDON · SINGAPORE · BEIJING · SHANGHAI · HONG KONG · TAIPEI · CHENNAI

Published by

World Scientific Publishing Co. Pte. Ltd.

5 Toh Tuck Link, Singapore 596224

USA office: 27 Warren Street, Suite 401-402, Hackensack, NJ 07601

UK office: 57 Shelton Street, Covent Garden, London WC2H 9HE

Library of Congress Cataloging-in-Publication Data
Preparing youths for the workplace / [edited by] Jessie Ee, Agnes Chang.
    pages cm
    Includes bibliographical references and index.
    ISBN 978-9814689458 (hardcover : alk. paper) -- ISBN 978-9814689465 (pbk. : alk. paper)
    1. School-to-work transition. 2. Career education. 3. Young adults--Employment. 4. Vocational
guidance. I. Ee, Jessie, editor of compilation, author. II. Chang, Agnes Shook Cheong, editor of
compilation, author.
    LC1037.P74 2015
    371.2'27--dc23

                                                             2015011289

British Library Cataloguing-in-Publication Data
A catalogue record for this book is available from the British Library.

Typeset by Stallion Press
Email: enquiries@stallionpress.com

Printed in Singapore

To succeed in work and win in life, youths today need to be self-motivated and resilient. They must have valuable soft skills and practise good values like integrity and a strong sense of responsibility. The future opens up for those who are trustworthy. The authors in this book have a thorough grasp of these important attributes. The book offers help and understanding to job seekers as well as educators who see their role as helping guide youths to suitable jobs and winning attitudes.

Mr Lim Siong Guan
Former Head of the Singapore Civil Service and Author of
"The Leader, The Teacher & You"

In today's expanding knowledge-based economy, organisations are raising the bar for new recruits. Rather than be complacent, schools, students, parents, and other stakeholders need to adapt to this rapidly changing working environment. Because young people bring a variety of strengths to the workforce, including creativity, adaptability, technology-savvy, and global awareness, it is thus critical that these are cultivated and nurtured. Divided into three parts, the book offers a broad spectrum of practical life skills and competencies, such as self-awareness and critical communication, which are essential and important in narrowing the skills gap in organisations. The book is an excellent resource of information for schools as the authors have provided real-life scenarios suited for healthy discussions in class, as well as some practice notes to perform when evaluating skills. I congratulate Jessie Ee and Agnes Chang for this timely edition.

Prof Tan Oon Seng
Director, National Institute of Education, Singapore

It is fairly common for many in the West to assert that what leads to greatest job satisfaction among workers in East Asia is the acquisition of 'the three Cs'; a condominium, a platinum credit card and a prestigious club membership. This valuable book challenges this view in no uncertain terms and offers a more humanistic perspective in arguing that when it comes to employment doing a job that is emotionally satisfying leads to greater happiness in the long run than the acquisition of a large bank balance.

In the first of two main sections the authors first stress the importance of first identifying one's strengths and weaknesses and provide excellent examples of how to set necessary goals to bring about a recognition of what needs to be done to effect improvement. The second longer section deals with various aspects of social and emotional learning and offers advice on how to develop a healthy work-life balance. This is a valuable practical book not only for today's youth about to enter employment but also for those currently in work who feel unfulfilled.

Prof Maurice Galton
Emeritus Professor, University of Cambridge

This ground-breaking book highlights the critical social-emotional competencies and work-related skills that prepare youth for productive, fulfilling career paths. The authors provide strong rationales for why these competencies are important and practical guidance on ways to develop them. Young people, parents, educators, and employers will all benefit from the insights and strategies shared in this informative volume.

Dr Roger P. Weissberg
University Distinguished Professor of Psychology and Education,
University of Illinois at Chicago, Chief Knowledge Officer,
Collaborative for Academic, Social,
and Emotional Learning (CASEL)

In *Preparing Youths for the Workplace*, Jessie Ee and Agnes Chang have brought together authors with a range of expertise across education and work, to create an informative resource book to support young people's transition to the workplace. The authors draw on their particular knowledge of Asia and experience of the global world of work. The chapters are written in everyday language for the intended audience of young people, parents, educators and employers with up-to-date material, self-questions for the reader and resources for those who wish to find out more. The book focuses on ways to enhance specific employability skills, especially the critical 'soft skills' employers expect. Young people can work through the book themselves, or parents and those who mentor young people can use the book as an excellent guide.

Dr Judith MacCallum
Associate Professor, School of Education, Murdoch University

During the life long process of establishing one's identity, such questions as "What kind of person am I?" beg answers along the way. The importance of self-awareness and a positive self-concept in the career planning and development process can never be overstated. Life is filled with ample opportunities for people to become aware of, explore, and develop personal interests, attitudes, and aptitudes. This book is timely in the sense that it provides valuable guidance on how students can develop a greater awareness and appreciation of themselves in relationship to others, school, and work. Featured with specific and realistic suggestions, the readers of the book will find it self-explanatory and self-sufficient.

Dr Mingming Zhou
Assistant Professor, Faculty of Education, University of Macau.

One important role of schools is to equip and prepare its students for the future — and that includes the important transition from school to the work place. This book is a timely and invaluable resource for educators and parents as they work with the young to build on their strengths and develop the necessary competencies and disposition to start strong when they begin work — and to be ready for a lifestyle where continual learning and upgrading is the norm.

Mr Winston Hodge
Principal, Anglo-Chinese School (Independent)
and former Principal of Raffles Junior College,
St Gabriel's Secondary as well as a former
Cluster Superintendent in the Ministry of Education's Headquarters

The world of work is evolving just as much as the world around us is changing. The half-life of change in our VUCA environment has shortened considerably as compared to the past generations. Our students of today may experience a greater cultural shock when they enter the workforce tomorrow. As such, the values, attitudes and skills that they are inculcated with from young are the foundation upon which they have to leverage on to help them pursue their careers as they join the workforce. This book is a boon as it provides parents and our youths with useful insights to help them transit from learning in an academic perspective to contributing in the work force as they step out into the world.

Mrs Elaine Quek
Principal, Maha Bodhi School

It's a great read, especially for potential job seekers and people giving advice to potential job seekers, as it identifies what the real world is about, and what employers are looking for, and how youths should taper their expectations. I have come across many different personalities in interviews, and I wish many of them would taper their expectations as it is not what the company can do for you, but what you can contribute to the company. No one is indispensable, and I believe this book is one of the ways to highlight the world out there isn't just about having the best grades, which will get you the best pay and employers lining up to hire you.

Mr Glenn Tan
Executive Director, Tan Chong International Ltd

The book provides useful insights into the practicalities and framework of an ever-growing need for industry knowledge and experience prior to the start of a career. It provides youths, undergraduates and young graduates from various levels with perspectives on pertinent and local contextual issues that need consideration. Knowing and managing specific industry related expectations are both prerequisites for a meaningful and significant orientation into a selected field of choice.

Mr Felix Lim
Director, Total Empowerment Pte Ltd

The book is good for ITE, polytechnic and the undergraduate students. As a parent, I find there are many useful tips that will assist me in preparing our children for tomorrow's world. I especially enjoyed reading on how we as parents can work with the school to shape our children's character.

Dr Julianah Abu-Wong
Parent and Gynecologist

A valuable and beneficial book with succinct points and easy-to-read for youths. We, youths are at the perplex stage of finding our own identity and life purpose. The book helps to equip us with social emotional skills such as self-awareness to better apprehend ourselves, preparing us for the highly competitive workplace with essential employability skills such as interview skills. I especially like how the book values and emphasizes the importance of one's personality and character over competencies and abilities. As a zealous and driven youth, I do agree at times we get blinded by our own needs and goals and lose ourselves along the way. A person who holds the right values and morals will be able to achieve the highest potential and have a fulfilling career. I would greatly recommend the book to my polytechnic friends preparing to enter the workplace.

Agnes Toh
Ngee Ann Polytechnic Student pursuing a Diploma in Early Childhood Education

In my perspective, this book definitely will enlighten many youths who are not sure about themselves. Many times, we, ITE students feel demoralised by the judgement from society, peers and family members. This will lead us to think negatively of ourselves, leading some of us to go astray. However, with the assistance of this book telling us how to be aware of our strengths and how we can achieve them, it has built my self-esteem and confidence in myself. The book also enlightens us on what we can achieve personally as it provides employability skills, time management and ways to overcome the challenges we face with step by step guidance. I believe it will prepare us for tomorrow's world. We need to discover ourselves. Are you up to it?

Ethan Ng
ITE College West Student pursuing a Diploma in French Culinary and Restaurant Management

Foreword

The book *Preparing Youths for the Workplace* is a timely publication to provide employers, educators, parents and students with the needed resource on the information and guide at this time when new changes are being introduced into education at all levels, especially for ITEs and polytechnics.

It is important for parents and students to realise that there are different pathways in education that can lead to meaningful and fulfilling careers.

The days when employers just focus on paper qualifications are over. Job advertisements often require work-related experiences. There are also other essential skills and knowledge required of job seekers to clinch a job interview, such as communication skills, resume writing and interview skills as well as etiquette.

The ability to hold down a job and get promoted depends on one's employability skills, social skills, social-emotional competencies, positive work attitudes, and relationship management.

Many students and their parents tend to place priorities on prestige and high pay in the search for jobs without paying much attention to crucial factors like interest and the strengths of the students.

There are 20 chapters in this book and they are contributed by an employer, educators from the universities, a polytechnic and an ITE as well as teachers from a primary and secondary school and a parent. The topics included are comprehensive, covering expectations of an employer and the roles played by educators, industries, institutions and parents in developing communication skills, internship, employability skills, social-emotional competencies, career guidance and positive attitudes. It is noticeable that students with special needs are also not neglected in the book. Students with some learning disorders like AD(H)D and ASD can also be helped to carve out meaningful and productive careers. In a tight labour market, every person can be encouraged and helped to be gainfully and meaningfully employed.

I would like to congratulate the writers and editors for the comprehensive and thoughtful book which will be a useful resource for all employers, educators, parents and students.

Hawazi Daipi
Senior Parliamentary Secretary
Ministry of Education and Ministry of Manpower, Singapore

Preface

According to Parker (2012) there is a skills gap in organisations because of the mismatch in manufacturing, construction, healthcare and STEM (science, technology, engineering and mathematics) fields. Furthermore, employers are observing a lack of critical soft skills such as communication, creativity, collaboration and critical thinking. In Singapore, the ASPIRE (Applied Study in Polytechnics and ITE Review) Committee was tasked to study how these applied education in the various tertiary institutions can be enhanced.

To secure an interview for a job and to stay employed in a competitive workforce, there is a need to go beyond having a valid certification of knowledge and/or technical skills. Employers in Singapore have often spoken of the lack of soft skills and global awareness in our young workers.

Social-emotional learning was introduced into schools in the early 2000s to increase self and social awareness in our students at all levels. Competency in social-emotional domains is one of the crucial components of employability skills. Employability skills are often hyped in writings on preparation for employment and on-job professional development. Academic, language, communication and technical knowledge and skills form a part of employability skills. Thinking and problem-solving skills constitute another component. However, one's ability to stay ahead and succeed in the workplace and life depends on our positive work attitude, integrity, cooperation, resiliency, independence, discretion, responsible decision making, and appropriate social skills and behaviour.

Employers often prefer to recruit employees who have work-related experiences. Hence, courses which include internship and work attachment give added advantage to these students/graduates. Internship is not uncommon in professional/vocational programmes such as medicine, law, nursing, engineering, education, accounting, and food and beverage. Polytechnics and institutes of technical education (ITEs) usually provide work attachment for their courses. Universities and colleges in the United States and Germany started introducing internship schemes in their undergraduate programmes many years ago.

Schools and institutions of higher learning need to be aware of the needs and expectations of employers in order to prepare their students for their entry into the work market. New applicants for jobs must know how to clinch an interview with a convincing resume and impress interviewers enough to consider offering them the job. Group project work and co-curricular activities (CCA) in schools are purposefully introduced to develop cooperative and collaborating skills, listening skills, negotiation skills, networking skills and social awareness. Career guidance counselling is provided in secondary schools and later on, in all polytechnics and ITEs to guide students in discovering their strengths and interests in their search for suitable courses and vocations. Parents also need to support their children and schools in their search for work which will assist in developing their children's talents and interests. A good salary alone may not be able to sustain a person in a job which holds little interest for him or her.

This book is written for students, educators, parents and employers so that the skills gap between industries' and organisations' needs and expectations and their prospective employees' training can be better bridged for greater work satisfaction and productivity.

The book is divided into three parts. Part 1 addresses the expectations of employers and the role played by vocational education. Part 2 focuses on developing one's social-emotional competencies, e.g., identifying one's own strengths and weaknesses, managing one's emotions, developing social awareness such as perspective-taking and empathy, recognising how to develop better relationships and making responsible decisions. Part 3 covers a broad spectrum of employability skills including the importance of career counselling, collaboration, communication skills, interviewing, networking, internship, positive work attitude, resiliency, and independence — and how these skills and positive traits can be inculcated in schools, higher institutions and the home to prepare youths in their job search and employability.

I trust this book will invigorate and empower everyone in their quest to narrow the skill gaps of themselves as well as the youths of tomorrow.

Jessie Ee and Agnes Chang

Reference

Parker, A. (2012). *Preparing Today's Youths for Tomorrow's Workplace*. Association for Talented Development. Retrieved from www.td.org/Publications/Magazines/TD/TD-Achieve/2012/12/

Acknowledgements

I would like to thank God for giving me the inspiration to write another book to enhance the crucial soft skills and work competencies necessary for the workforce. The book is also dedicated to all youths and young undergraduates who are searching for their identity and strengths in securing their careers. Special thanks go to all the authors who have contributed to this book, as well as to Mr Hawazi Daipi, Senior Parliamentary Secretary, Ministry of Education and Ministry of Manpower for his encouragement and willingness to write the foreword in spite of his busy schedule. I would also like to thank my reviewers for their encouraging comments. Last but not least, thanks are due to my co-editor, Dr Agnes Chang, who mooted this idea in the first place, and to the capable staff of World Scientific Pte Ltd, especially Mr Chua Hong Koon and Ms Elizabeth Lie for their patience, insightful editing and timely printing of the book.

About the Contributors

Chang Shook Leng, Adelaide

Ms Adelaide Chang was educated at Pennsylvania State University, US, where she received both her Bachelor of Science and Master of Education degrees. A recipient of seven scholarships and study grants from the university, she has been involved in the fields of human resource management and human resource development upon her return to Singapore. For the last 35 years, she has coordinated recruitment exercises not only in Singapore but also in the Philippines, Hong Kong, Myanmar and India. Shook Leng has worked in statutory boards, government-linked companies and local multinational enterprises where she was sent to work in Brunei Darussalam in a senior management capacity. Training-wise, she has facilitated courses in job search and interviewing skills for the Community Development Councils and other community groups in the Henderson area. Besides topics on recruitment and interviewing skills, she has also facilitated programmes on financial literacy, leadership and communication skills. She holds the Advanced Certificate in Training and Assessment (ACTA) and Diploma in Adult and Continuing Education (DACE) under the Workforce Skills Qualifications (WSQ) Framework.

Chang Shook Cheong, Agnes

Dr Agnes Chang is currently an academic advisor to KLC International Institute which specialises in the training of pre-school teachers and principals as well as hospitality management personnel. She was lecturing at the National Institute of Education (NIE), National Technological University (NTU), from 1975 to 2010 and was its Associate Dean from 2000 to 2003. She was an Associate Professor when she retired in 2010.

Her major areas of research include motivation, bilingualism, critical thinking, creative problem solving, metacognition, employability and social emotional competencies, and she has lectured and published extensively on these topics. From 1999 to 2003, she was President of the Singapore Educational Research Association. She has been invited as a consultant to organisations in China, Hong Kong, Malaysia, Macau, Vietnam, Taiwan and the United States.

Chew Chelsea

Dr Chelsea Chew is a lecturer at NIE, NTU. She teaches and has taught courses on psychological disorders, self-regulation, educational psychology, individual differences and counselling. Dr Chew also supervises teacher trainees in their teaching practice, psychologists-in-training in educational assessment, and counsellors-in-training in case management. Prior to joining NIE, Dr Chew worked as a behavioural therapist and later in the School Health Service as a psychologist where she saw school-going children with learning, emotional and behavioural issues. She left to pursue her doctorate in educational psychology at the University of Queensland. She had short stints at schools in Queensland, the Dyslexia Association of Singapore and the Child Guidance Clinic. Dr Chew has worked with a number of students with attention deficit hyperactivity disorder (AD(H)D) and has an intimate knowledge of the strengths individuals with AD(H)D possess and the difficulties they face. Her key research areas include AD(H)D, bullying and self-regulation.

Chia Melvin

Mr Melvin Chia is a Certified Master Behavioural Consultant with The Institute of Motivational Living (United States) in Singapore and Asia, and is a specialist in the DISC Personality System; serving many school sectors through the use of personality, learning and motivational profiling tools. He has been coaching youths, educators and corporate partners since 2009. He specialises in executive coaching, life coaching, performance and career coaching. With his passion to discover and develop the potential of youths, he has mentored and made a difference in their lives, inculcating the STAR values of Strengths, Tenacity, Attitudes and Responsibility in each process. This, he strongly feels, is pivotal in nurturing today's youths to be accountable leaders of our future generation. He has been involved in youth work for more than 15 years.

Chiok Hwee Fen

Ms Chiok Hwee Fen is a teacher from Corporation Primary School. She has been teaching in this school for four years. Being a teacher for four years and counting, she has come to realise that education is much more than just delivering the contents in textbooks. The character building and holistic development of a child are all in our nurturing hands. As we embark on our journey as an educator, it is of paramount importance that we have the expertise to prepare students with navigation skills so that they can analyse situations, apply what they know to solve problems, imagine and invent new possibilities, and chart their own paths in their future workplaces.

Ee Jessie

Dr Jessie Ee is an educational psychologist and certified Behavioural Career Consultant with J Psychconsultancy. She is also an associate faculty of Singapore Institute of Management University (UniSIM) and NIE, NTU. She was formerly an Associate Professor in Psychological Studies in NIE. She has been involved with teacher education for over 27 years. She has a PhD scholarship from NIE and obtained her PhD specialising in educational psychology from the University of Newcastle, Australia. Her Masters degree was with the National University of Singapore (NUS) in the area of special education while she majored in English and Psychology for her BA and special education for her B. Ed degree. She has also been affiliated as a visiting scholar at Simon Fraser University, the University of Illinois in Chicago and Murdoch University in 2010. Her latest research addresses the impact of social-emotional learning as foundation skills for resilience and self-regulatory processes as well as the pedagogy skills of teachers. She has written over 138 published articles in referred journals, book chapters and professional conference papers. Among her books published to date are *Thinking about Thinking: What Educators Need to Know* (2004), *Empowering Metacognition through Social-Emotional Learning: Lessons for the Classroom* (2009), *Problem-based Learning: Lessons for the Classroom*

(2009) and *Infusing Thinking and Social-Emotional Learning for Children and Youths* (2012). She sits on the editorial board of several refereed journals including *Higher Ability Studies Journal* and *International Journal of Emotional Education*. Her research interests include pedagogy skills, social-emotional learning, resilience, self-regulation, metacognition, goal theory, motivation, problem-based learning and learning difficulties.

Lee Mun Kin, Joel

Upon graduating with a BSc (Hons) degree from the NUS Department of Microbiology, Dr Joel Lee was awarded a Glaxo-Institute of Molecular and Cell Biology (IMCB) scholarship to pursue his PhD studies at the Institute of Neurology, University College London, United Kingdom. He subsequently returned to Singapore to serve a five-year bond as a Research Fellow at the IMCB, Singapore's first biomedical sciences research institute, before being appointed as IMCB's Chief-of-Staff overseeing and coordinating both its administrative and research operations. He participated in Singapore's Genetic Modification Advisory Committee, and the Ministry of Education Working Committee on Life Sciences Education reviewing the GCE "O" and "A" level biology syllabus, amongst others. As its founding director, Dr Lee moved from IMCB to establish the School of Chemical and Life Sciences (SCL) in Nanyang Polytechnic in 2000. SCL has to date an annual intake of about 1,500 students over three years covering seven other diploma courses. Dr Lee was involved in supporting the Applied Study in Polytechnics and ITE Review (ASPIRE) Committee 3 (RC3) which was tasked to strengthen linkages between post-secondary education institutions (i.e., the polytechnics and ITE) and industry by having lead institutions drive industry engagement and partnerships along industry verticals. In the process, he was involved in launching an enhanced internship programme with two biologics manufacturing MNCs, i.e. GSK Biologicals and Novartis BiopharmOps for Nanyang Polytechnic's Diploma in Biologics and Process Technology students and is working out the details for other initiatives to prepare students to be "work ready" and equipped with deep skills relevant to their jobs subsequently and for lifelong learning.

Liew Eden

Mr Eden Liew was trained in marine engineering and started his career in the Republic of Singapore Navy's technical department. Since then, he has moved on to various administrative posts in several hospitals and government agencies including the Economic Development Board and Ministry of Education. He was also in the pioneering teams for the setting up of Nanyang Polytechnic and Republic Polytechnic. Five years ago he was appointed Principal of the Institute of Technical Education College East.

Lim Boon Huat

Dr Lim Boon Huat is currently Managing Director of Rohde & Schwarz Asia — a global hub of Rohde & Schwarz which is the world leader in the field of wireless testing and measurement, broadcasting, secured communication and radio monitoring. Dr Lim started in Rohde & Schwarz Singapore's operation in 1997. Over the last 17 years, he grew the Singapore operation from scratch to a 400-staff full-fledged global operation. Dr Lim also sits on the Board of Directors of many of Rohde & Schwarz's subsidiaries in China, Germany, Singapore and Malaysia. In addition, he also serves as a member on the Board of Governors of Institute of Technical Education (ITE), as an advisory member in Nanyang Polytechnic's School of Engineering, and in the NUS's Department of Electrical and Computer Engineering. In 2014, he was appointed co-chair of one of the three ASPIRE committees to look into the work-based learning in polytechnics and ITEs. Prior to joining Rohde & Schwarz, Dr Lim held various appointments in the Singapore Economic Development Board where he was involved in small and medium enterprise (SME) development, industry development and the promotion of international direct investment. Dr Lim graduated in Germany with a degree in engineering under a public service commission (PSC) scholarship in 1986. He has a PhD in business management from the University of South Australia, an MBA from Warwick Business School and an MSC (Finance) from the City University of New York.

Lui Brian

Mr Brian Lui has been teaching since 1993 and specialises in physical education (PE). He is currently the Head of Department (HOD) for PE and Curricular Activities in Northland Secondary School, but was also the HOD of Character and Citizenship Education from 2010 to 2012. He is passionate about teaching students and believes that every child is precious and with care and guidance, every child will succeed in life. His other passion is in sports and he has developed Northland into a powerhouse in hockey and floorball, where his teams have won over 200 awards over the last 20 years. In his personal life, he participates in all kinds of sports, from hockey to scuba diving to running marathons. In 2013, Mr Lui was awarded the Outstanding Physical Education Teacher Award (OPETA), a testimony to his good work in the development of students through physical education. He has shared on "Leveraging on PE to inculcate Values and 21st Century Competencies" at the 2013 PE and Sports Education Conference as well as on "Values, Character and Leadership Education through Sports CCAs" at the 2014 Teachers' Conference.

Mok Jeffrey

Dr Jeffrey Mok has over 20 years' experience in teaching and training tertiary students and adults in communication skills. He has taught students in polytechnics and universities not just in Singapore but also in Japan and Hong Kong. He has also conducted training in communication skills to government officials, private corporations and educators in several parts of Asia. He has published many articles and chapters including co-authoring an English workbook for Japanese university students, *Celebrating around the World*. He is currently an associate director and lecturer in the Centre for English Language and Communication, NUS. His doctorate in education is from Leicester University, United Kingdom and he has a Master of Education (English Language Teaching) from Sheffield University, United Kingdom. His research interests are in English language and communication skills with special focus on e-learning, learning methodologies, curriculum matters and distributed cognition.

Siah Siew Ling

Ms Siah Siew Ling has been in the teaching profession for 11 years. As a School Staff Developer in Corporation Primary School, she graduated with a BA (Diploma in Education) at the National Institute of Education. Her role as a School Staff Developer is to help every teacher to continually progress in their journey of professional growth and help establish a culture of a collaborative community so as to achieve school and pupil outcomes. As a planner and designer for training and a champion for learning which caters to the different learning needs of her teachers, she also leads and mentors different teams of teachers and takes an active interest in sharing her experiences and expertise to motivate them to build their capacity. She believes that as a fraternity, it is important to continue to work at building the professional capacity of teachers as they are the key to the learning and development of pupils and to passing on the torch of learning to the next generation. Her clarity of purpose and her belief to dream that she can touch the life of every student keeps her going, growing and glowing. She will continue to nurture the Hearts, design learning programmes (Head) and deliver engaging lessons (Hands) to her students so that they can find purpose in life and live to be active citizens. She believes that if she can reach the students of today, she will touch the children of tomorrow.

Tan Esther

Dr Esther Tan has over 40 years of working experience in the fields of education and counselling as a teacher in Hong Kong, a counsellor in Canada and a teacher educator in Singapore. As Head of psychological studies at NIE (1990 to 2003), she spearheaded counselling training for teachers and psychologists. Currently she is an adjunct professor at UniSIM engaged in developing and teaching counsellor education programmes at both the undergraduate and post-graduate level. To date she has published 60 journal papers and four books: *Counselling Pupils* (1983), *Winning Ways with Teens: A Practical Guide for Parents* (1997), *Counselling in Schools: Theories, Processes and Techniques* (2004) and *What Do I Say to My Net-Savvy Kids?: Internet Safety Issues for Parents* (2006). Her other professional contributions include serving on the Management Committee of Singapore Psychological Society and teaching as a visiting professor at ITE College East. Active in community services, Dr Tan was a founder member of Students Care Service and served on its board for 30 years (1979 to 2009). She sat on the Panel of Advisors to the Juvenile Court for 30 years (1979 to 2010) and is the current Chairperson of SAGE Counselling Centre. She is the recipient of three National Day awards (PB in 1986, PBM in 1993 and BBM in 2006) and has been appointed Justice of the Peace since 1998.

Tan Ian

Ian Tan is Founder and Chief Enabling Officer of Lifeskills Resources Pte Ltd and Lifeskills Enrichment Pte Ltd, two dynamic educational and training consultancy firms that help transform individuals, teams and organisations by providing human capital solutions and assessment tools to unlock the potential in people. Ian holds a degree in social science and applied psychology and a Master of Guidance and Counselling. He is a Certified Harrison Assessments Profiler, Certified Strong Interest Inventory Facilitator and Certified Workplace Big Five Consultant. He is also an accredited facilitator for two powerful leadership tools, the Leadership Practices Inventory (LPI) of the Leadership Challenge Model and the Multifactor Leadership Questionnaire (MLQ) of the Full Range Leadership Model. His special interests in research, training and consultancy are in the fields of human potential, leadership, psychology, learning and personal effectiveness.

Tan John

Dr John Tan is currently a senior lecturer at the Physical Education and Sports Science Academic Group, NIE. He has a doctoral degree in sports biomechanics from Loughborough University (1997) and engages in sports at a variety of levels. He was involved in developing the Singapore Badminton Association's 'Modified Badminton' programme (2004–2008) for primary school children and instructed judo at St Joseph's Institution (SJI) from 1977 to 1994. He was also the national coach for the high jump from 1993 to 1999. He conducts research in the mechanics of running and jumping. and lectures for the Singapore Sports Council in their National Coaches Accreditation Programme and for the Singapore Civil Defence Force in their physical instructor courses. Dr Tan was a member of Singapore's Olympic Pathway Programme (2004–2012) that advised on the development of athletes for the Olympic Games. He was a member of NTU and SJI Sports Advisory Committees and is currently a member of the SAF Fitness Advisory Board.

Tan Khye Suan

Mr Tan Khye Suan has been an Executive Director of the MCYC Community Services Society (MCYC) since 2002. He is married and has three children who have all completed post-secondary education and are currently pursuing tertiary education in various universities. Before joining the social work sector, Mr Tan was a qualified town planner who worked in the building industry, both in the public and private sector for 18 years. In the last 13 years at MCYC, Mr Tan has worked with children, youths and their parents in the community and in school-based social work. He runs programmes and seminars, as well as counsels children, youths and parents. He has covered various areas of family life, including delinquent and anti-social behaviours, mental health and developmental issues, marital and relationship problems, and parenting issues. MCYC is now a significant partner with various government authorities in children, youth and parenting services, having grown from employing nine to over 70 staff members over the last 13 years. Mr Tan holds a Bachelor of Arts (Economics and Statistics) and a Graduate Diploma in Social Work from NUS, and a Master of Arts (Town and Regional Planning) from University of Sheffield, United Kingdom.

Contents

Foreword   xi

Preface   xiii

Acknowledgements   xvii

About the Contributors   xix

Part 1:   Introduction   1

1.   Preparing for Work, Equipping for the Future   3
     Lim Boon Huat

2.   Why Youths Need to Be Prepared for Work   25
     Eden Liew

Part 2:   Developing Social-Emotional Competencies for Life   35

3.   Understanding Oneself through Self-Awareness   37
     Jessie Ee

4.   Managing and Regulating Emotions   45
     Jessie Ee

5.   Developing and Promoting Social Awareness   57
     Jessie Ee

6. Relationship Management   65
     Jessie Ee

7. Making Responsible Decisions   77
     Jessie Ee

**Part 3:   Developing Work-Related Competencies
             at Home and in School   89**

8. Knowing Oneself and Career Counselling   91
     Ian Tan & Melvin Chia

9. Getting the Most out of Industry Internships   101
     Joel Lee

10. Employability Skills in Career Preparation   111
     Agnes Chang

11. Networking through Collaborative Learning   119
     Agnes Chang

12. Building Confidence and Resilience   125
     Esther Tan

13. Fostering Critical Communication Skills for the Future   135
     Jeffrey Mok

14. Sharpening Your Resume Writing and Interview Skills   149
     Adelaide Chang

15. Work Values Through Sports   163
     John Tan

16. Preparing Our Children for Tomorrow's World   173
     Tan Khye Suan

17. Preparing Future-Ready Students: A Teacher's Perspective   183
     Brian Lui

18. Nurturing Primary Students for the Real World 199
    Siah Siew Ling & Chiok Hwee Fen

19. Self-Regulation of AD(H)D Habits 211
    Chelsea Chew

20. Using Positive Psychology to Help Young Adults
    with High Functioning Autism Transit
    to the Workplace 223
    Chelsea Chew

Part 1

Introduction

Chapter 1

Preparing for Work, Equipping for the Future

Lim Boon Huat

Success in one's life and career does not come by chance. Very often we have to plan and prepare for it. Having passion, dreams and aspirations are not enough. We must take personal action to prepare for our career journey. It may take a long time to establish a successful career but as the Chinese saying goes, "a thousand miles begins with the first step". It is never too early to start this step while in school. Having an early and good career preparation is important if we want to secure a winning chance to fulfil our career aspiration in the current globalised and hyper-competitive world.

The need for, and significance of, good career preparation is well acknowledged today within the education sector. Boosted by the recent government's initiative to make our education system more relevant to meet the changing needs of industry, our youths can look forward to a more supportive environment today to advance their career ambitions. Such an environment will give them a good starting point in their career journey.

One key factor that enhances the relevance of education to the needs of industry is to encourage applied learning in schools and tertiary institutions. The main goal is to strengthen development of deep skills and workplace competencies among students so as to better prepare them for the workplace. Endorsing this idea, Prime Minister Lee Hsien Loong announced at the opening of a new Institute of Technology (ITE) campus in January 2014 the setup of a review committee (ASPIRE — Applied Study in Polytechnics and ITE Review) involving key stakeholders to examine ways to enhance and implement applied learning in ITEs and polytechnics and possibly extending to the universities. The recommendations of the ASPIRE committee were submitted and accepted by the government in August 2014. The work of ASPIRE has provided the basis for the establishment of SkillsFuture, which is a high-level national movement chaired by Deputy Prime Minister Tharman Shanmugaratnam. It aims to foster closer linkages and integration between education, industry and workforce development to promote greater skills mastery in every vocation so as to enhance the capability of our workforce.

Underpinning the applied learning initiative is the desire to enhance the employability of local tertiary graduates. Towards this objective, one key recommendation is to strengthen acquisition of deep and complex skills and workplace competencies by providing more opportunities for students to get more exposure to the workplace through industry attachments and internship. Through this initiative, local tertiary students and graduates would then stand a good chance to compete and thrive effectively in the increasingly competitive job market.

While education and industry are making changes to further enhance applied learning, our students must also take ownership to embrace this change. They must make proactive efforts to develop industry-relevant skills and competencies to enhance their own career journey. To do this they must understand what it means to build up one's career or vocation and define strategies towards this goal.

Although the need to develop their career is well understood, many young people often struggle to make the right career choice due to lack of information and understanding of the working world. Without a clear goal in mind they are not able to prepare for work early.

In this chapter, I will explain why it is important for school leavers and tertiary students to (1) take ownership of their own career development and (2) to start building their career journey early while they are still in school. A key part in preparing for work is to understand the realities of job markets and what employers look for in young talents. To prepare for the working world there are some practical strategies that students can take to strengthen the necessary skills for a successful career in the future.

Transiting to the Job Market

Making the right career choice is one issue facing our youth today. For many school leavers, making the transition to tertiary education can be quite daunting. Suddenly, they are confronted with the need to choose a course of specialisation in polytechnics or ITEs. They have to think very hard about their career choices given the very limited knowledge and exposure they have about the various jobs and workplaces. Often they resort to friends, parents and relatives for advice about the various job options in order to decide what course to take in polytechnics or ITEs. For some, they simply follow the choice of their friends. Others have no choice but to base their decision on the entry-points requirements of the course. From my own informal survey, only very few students actually apply for a course based on their self-defined career direction.

After students have chosen and enrolled in a course, they do not really give much serious thought to their personal career planning and development. They assume that by completing the course well with good grades, they will stand a good chance of getting a good job in the job market. However, as they soon discover, it is not so straightforward. Getting an educational qualification may not necessarily lead to a good job. Many graduates on an average take about six months to find a job, and for the not so fortunate ones, it could take even longer. For the first time many begin to realise that getting the desired job is not as easy as they have originally thought. Competition in the job market is very keen. Fresh graduates are not just competing with fellow fresh graduates from their cohort but also with experienced people in the market. It becomes clear to them beyond grades there are other subjective factors that will determine whether one gets a job. Being highly educated academically is no longer adequate for work.

Or some may find that there is not much demand in the job market for what they are trained for. As an integral part of an economic system, the job market is subject to swings in demand and supply. Either one ends up in a situation where there is no demand for a particular profession due to industry restructuring or in a situation where there is an oversupply of graduates for a particular profession. In today's society, economic uncertainty is rampant — not only jobs but entire industries could disappear overnight. For example in the IT industry, technology changes so fast that by the time one graduates, the knowledge acquired in school may have already become obsolete. The oversupply situation happens when students choose courses of study because of its popularity, perceived prestige and good pay in the sector.

Realities of the Job Market

Indeed, the realities of the job market is something many young graduates find hard to grapple with, especially when they have not been well exposed to the working world. The job market is subject to economic cycle, globalisation, technology and socio-political changes, and is often volatile, driven by business expansion, restructuring or contraction. We are living in an increasingly volatile, uncertain, complex and ambiguous (VUCA) environment. Such swings have become part and parcel of working life for any participants in the economy.

Globalisation has also resulted in geopolitical borders declining in relevance to global business practices. Global corporations are showing less loyalty to countries of origin and more to regions in which they find new markets. The modern multinational organisation has evolved far beyond a collection of country-based subsidiaries to become instead a globally integrated array of specialised business functions — procurement, management, R&D, manufacturing, sales, etc. — distributed through the world, wherever attractive markets exist and talents can be found.

The knowledge economy is also demanding new types of learners and creators leading to new forms of learning and education. The proportion of American workers doing jobs that call for complex and deep skills has grown three times as fast as employment in general (The Economist, 2006). Driven by technology and competition, there has been a trend towards "massification" of education in the last few decades. More and more people, especially in the developing economies, have now access to higher education. Many see education as the way to improve their economic livelihood. Almost 17 million students worldwide earned first university degrees in 2010, with about 5.5 million of these in the science and engineering fields. The growth of students in higher education comes mainly from developing economies. In 2007, China overtook the United States as the world leader in the number of doctoral degrees awarded in the natural sciences and engineering with an increase from about 4,000 in 1996 to more than 31,000 in 2010. In Asia, China has been the largest producer of science and engineering degrees since 2000 (National Science Board, 2014).

The "massification" of education (Trow, 2000) coupled with the mobility of international talents, have led to an increasing influx of young and highly educated graduates not only from developing countries but also from those stagnant economies in developed countries, entering the global workforce. What all these means is that competition in the job market especially from developing countries, will be very keen. Having an open economy and being a global hub, Singapore is limited in what it can do to stop this influx.

Multinational employers do not show loyalty to any country when it comes to hiring people, unless they are restricted by local labour regulations. This means that employers now have more choices beyond the local graduates. It should also be noted that employers do not necessarily have special consideration for fresh graduates as a category by itself in their hiring practice. They will look for the best fit among the wide choices of candidates to fill their available positions. Ultimately, the position is given based on many factors such as pay expectation, experience, and personal attributes.

Employers also place a premium on expertise. For many employers, work experience is a good proxy for expertise. The reason is that having work experience helps to reduce the overall investment in training to bring the newcomer on board. We should also note that having attained a good educational qualification does not necessary equate to expertise. Hence, doctors and lawyers must complete one year of training praxis in a hospital or law firm before they can practise their profession. Knowing the importance of gaining expertise, many well-informed fresh graduates are looking for opportunities to secure a job to allow them to practise their profession. For those who are unable to find jobs relevant to their educational qualification, there is a possibility that they may end up in jobs that do not commensurate in pay and position with their qualification. In this respect, although educational qualification continues to be a key criterion, deep skills and practical experience have become even more crucial for employers in hiring.

While vacancies are filled mostly by recruiting from the job market, increasingly it is now filled by tapping into companies' talent pipelines. Progressive companies are always on the lookout for good talents within their ranks and people they come into contact with to form their talent pipeline for future positions. Having a talent pipeline helps to reduce companies' recruitment and talent search cost. Therefore, informal contacts with industry via internship or projects could provide our students with invaluable opportunities for future employment. Given the importance of expertise and experience, it is therefore important that students should learn to value work experience in their career preparation. Whenever possible, they should secure a chance to gain relevant working experience.

Common Gaps in Local Students and Fresh Graduates As Observed by Employers

Many of our local graduates often fail to appreciate the realities of the job market. They fail to realise that having an educational qualification or good grades alone is not a guarantee to secure a position and that career success is based not so much on obtaining a higher degree such as a Masters or PhD but on a person's work credentials and track record in the industry. The days when employees could go to their employers to ask for pay increase after obtaining an additional educational qualification are over. Pay in most organisations (public or private) is now based on work performance and contribution and no longer on academic credentials.

From the numerous job interviews conducted in our firm, we note that in many instances students and graduates are also not so well prepared for the workplace. They do not understand the intricacies of the working world. This is probably due to their lack of exposure. This is perfectly understandable as they have been socialised since childhood in a school and academic environment that has its own organisational cultures and knowledge practices. For them, the school is their only social reality of an organisation.

The practices of the workplace are certainly very different from that of schools. It is not surprising that many things in the workplace which working adults take for granted are something new and surprising for young students. For example, many students do not know how a company functions and how the various departments interact in the operation of a company. One intern innocently admits that she does not know what people are doing in front of computers in an office!

Many are also applying for jobs in the industry without knowing much about the industry, the markets and its ecosystems. For example, engineering graduates are not able to name the common brands of instruments or tools used for engineering practice in their domain. They have also seldom worked with industry technical specifications or data sheets in their engineering assignments or project case studies.

There is also a mismatch of expectation in terms of graduates' domain knowledge. Potential employers would expect that after three years of education in a specialised domain, graduates would have developed in-depth understanding of the domains. Unfortunately this is not the case. As noted in various interviews, many fresh graduates do not seem to demonstrate mastery of their core domain. They may have a wide "vocabulary" of the subjects but their understanding of their subjects is found to be superficial, fragmented and disconnected. Employers are often not impressed by the "vocabulary". They are more interested in candidates who have the maturity of thought and have developed personal and practical insights into their domain knowledge. The reasons for this gap may be attributed to the fact that most students learn in order to pass exams. Once they clear the exams the knowledge is "shelved".

Another reason is attributed to the fact that learning in some schools is very much focused and prioritised on acquiring facts and conceptual knowledge. In recent years there has also been a trend towards broadening the course curriculum due to the schools' desire to enhance employability of their graduates. Consequently there are not many opportunities to develop deeper understanding of the subject given the limited time frame. Given that the subjects are taught in separate modules, there are also not enough opportunities for students to pull what they learn together into a practice.

Acquiring Work Experience

Many would argue that all these observations stem from lack of working experience on the part of students and graduates. This fact is implicitly known, but what constitutes working experience is often not well understood. We tend to talk about work experience in general terms and this does not help the students much in grasping it. Consequently they do not know the specific gaps in job experience they need to close. Work experience essentially boils down to the individual's tacit and situated understanding of the various aspects of work in the workplace. In acquiring work experience, we can use as proxy for work experience, the list of workplace competencies by Eraut *et al.* (2005) in his study of the learning trajectory of professionals in their early careers as shown in Table 1.1.

Preparing for work thus involves immersing in a work context and collecting practical experience in these areas. The role of context in learning is important but unfortunately it is often underappreciated. There is a tendency in teaching to decontexualise concepts into theories and frameworks. According to contextual learning theory (Imel, 2000), learning is a sense-making process (Weick, 1995; Devin, 1998) and it occurs when students process new knowledge in such a way that it makes sense to them in their own frames of reference. It assumes that the mind naturally seeks meaning in context, that is, in relation to the person's current environment, and that it does so by searching for relationships that make sense and appear useful.

Reason for the Gap as Observed by Employers

These abovementioned gaps are rather prevalent among young students and graduates. We can always attribute the observed gaps to lack of working

Table 1.1   A Typology of Workplace Learning Trajectories

Task Performance	*Rote Performance*
Speed and fluency	Prioritisation
Complexity of tasks and problems	Range of responsibility
Range of skills required	Supporting other people's learning
Communication with a wide range of people	Leadership
Collaborative work	Accountability
	Supervisory role
	Delegation
Awareness and Understanding	Handling ethical issues
Other people: colleagues, customers, managers, etc.	Coping with unexpected problems
	Crisis management
Contexts and situations	Keeping up-to-date
One's own organisation	
Problems and risks	*Teamwork*
Priorities and strategic issues	Collaborative work
Value issues	Facilitating social relations
	Joint planning and problem solving
Personal Development	Ability to engage in and promote mutual learning
Self evaluation	
Self management	
Handling emotions	
Building and sustaining relationships	*Decision Making and Problem Solving*
Disposition to attend to other perspectives	When 10 seek expert help
Disposition to consult and work with others	Dealing with complexity
	Group decision making
Disposition to team and improve one's practice	Problem analysis
	Formulating and evaluating options
Accessing relevant knowledge and expertise	Managing the process within an appropriate timescale
Ability to learn from experience	Decision making under pressure
Academic Knowledge and Skills	*Judgement*
Use of evidence and argument	Quality of performance output and outcomes
Accessing formal knowledge	
Research-based practice	Priorities
Theoretical thinking	Value issues
Knowing what you might need to know	Levels of risk
Using knowledge resources (human paper-based, electronic)	
Learning how to use relevant theory in a range of practical situations	

Source: Eraut *et al.*, 2005.

experience but on deeper analysis, there is more to it than simply not having the work exposure. Underlying this issue are some misconceptions and attitudes among students about work and study, and as long as these misconceptions are not clarified and resolved these observed gaps will be perpetuated.

Besides being ignorant about work realities, many of our students also often do not pay much attention to the question of preparing for work. Ironically they may enrol in the course of study to learn a profession yet they do not see the need to learn *about* the profession. They assume that the course is adequate to launch them into a career.

There may be students who recognise the need to prepare for work but they do not see the necessity of preparing for work early. They would still choose to focus on completing their studies first and leave the work preparation to the time when they enter the workforce.

Underlying these scenarios are the misconceptions that (1) education is fully adequate to prepare students for work and (2) the preparation for work can be deferred to the time when one enters the workforce. In both cases this has led to the observed gaps illustrated above.

Complementing Education and Workplace

To address these misconceptions, students and fresh graduates need to better understand and appreciate the differences between education and workplace in preparing one for work. Both play an important role in one's career preparation but offer different aspects of training.

Having a good education is first and foremost very important for one's career development. The school provides an excellent environment to transfer essential knowledge required in the workplace efficiently and in a structured manner which otherwise may not be possible in the workplace. It also provides a lot of opportunities and time for student's cognitive development. However, schools do have limitations in preparing students for work in real life.

Schools and workplaces differ in their epistemic culture. Epistemic culture refers generally to the styles of thinking, believing and acting with respect to knowledge. It shapes and structures work practices and approaches to learning within a domain. In many schools' epistemic culture, the system is organised for creation, efficient transfer and testing of academic and domain knowledge. The goal is to equip students to be conversant with knowledge and concepts in various disciplines to enable them to apply their understanding in practice later in the profession. With its focus on cognitive development, the system inevitably emphasises theory over practice or head knowledge over skills (mind over body). Students going through their years of education in this mode are thus socialised to the life of an academic.

In this respect, no matter how authentic the learning environment in school may be, it will never be able to replace the real work environment. In the training of any vocation or profession we have to reckon that work is a vital component in learning. Recognising this, Germany, which has a highly successful model for training a highly skilled workforce, emphasises the importance of being trained *for* and *by* work.

The epistemic culture of the workplace is very different compared to that of the school. The workplace is organised for the production of goods and services to create entrepreneurial profit. Unlike schools or universities where the primary goal is knowledge transfer and creation, the focus in the workplace is on practice. Practice is part and parcel of organisational life. Every workplace has its own form of practice. Although the term "practice" is used often in medicine and law, it is a generic term applicable to all work settings to denote a structured social space with its own rules of engagement, web of relationships, values, authorities and legitimacy. Unlike academia, workplaces vis-à-vis industry practitioners adopt a more pragmatic and utility perspective of knowledge. For them, knowledge is not an end in itself. They recognise practice as the starting and ending point for knowledge. Often this fact is not so well understood by academics and students.

Many educators often hold the view that it is theory that informs practice and for them the workplace is a place for the application of theories learned in school. Under this assumption, the students should therefore be equipped with as much knowledge as possible to prepare them for practice. It should be noted that today, academia is no longer the only producers of knowledge. The workplace has also become a major contributor and producer of knowledge in terms of technology innovation and intellectual properties, and the pace is increasing. New types of knowledge and practices are constantly created, modified and evolved in the workplace. Some of the knowledge domains such as software engineering, production technology or supply chain management currently taught in higher education originally arose out of workplace practice. In some professions nearly all new practices are both invented and developed in the workplace, with the role of academia being confined to that of dissemination, evaluation and post-hoc construction of theoretical rationales. Hence in many cases it is the practice that informs theory.

Very few people would also associate the workplace with a place of learning. This is because we tend to see learning as educating the mind and as conceptual knowledge acquisition. In fact, the workplace is also a place where a lot of formal and informal learning is taking place. Beyond a physical location, the workplace also has a social-cultural dimension of shared meaning, ideology, interpersonal relationships, ideas and attitudes. Therefore, learning to work means also learning to thrive in this social, cultural and political environment. However, many students are not well prepared socially for the workplace as they interact mostly with fellow students of the same age group in a structured school setting. Many struggle with relating to people of different age groups and handling ambiguous tasks and various uncertainties typical in any work setting.

Unlike in a school setting, learning in the workplace is often informal and implicit. It is learned through participation and involvement in a series of learning episodes that builds towards one's competencies. The various forms of learning are illustrated in Table 1.2.

Development of Expertise

The transition from predominantly explicit learning in a school environment to implicit learning in the workplace is one major adjustment to be made. The adjustment calls for a shift towards more integrated and contextual learning that focuses on developing one's emotional and social intelligence. While noting that there are various ways of learning these competencies in the workplace, students and early career professionals

Table 1.2　A Typology of Early Career Learning Processes and Activities

Work processes with learning as a by-product	Learning activities located within work or learning processes	Learning processes at or near the workplace
Participation in group processes	Asking questions	Being supervised
Working alongside others	Listening	Being coached
Consultation	Observing	Being mentored
Tackling challenging tasks and roles	Getting information	Shadowing
Problem solving	Learning from mistakes	Visiting other sites
Trying things out	Reflecting	Independent study
Consolidating, extending and refining skills	Locating resource people	Conferences
Work with clients	Giving and receiving feedback	Short courses
		Working for a qualification

Source: Eraut *et al.*, 2007.

often do not know what it takes to achieve mastery in their profession and specifically, how a proficient person would execute their work and tasks differently from them.

The development of expertise from novice to expert level takes time. As shown in the model by Dreyfus on the different levels of expertise (see Table 1.3), differences in performance are largely attributed to an intimate understanding of the interplay between knowledge and the work context.

To become proficient, more situated awareness and tacit understanding are increasingly required. In order to achieve a higher level of proficiency, it is important for the student to take personal ownership of his or her learning (self-directed learning) and change the mode of learning from that found in the school environment.

Benefits of Preparing for, and Learning about, Work Early

Given the limits of what education institutions can do in preparing for real world practice, it does make sense to start early in preparing for work while in school rather than to defer it to after graduation. There are also many good reasons why students should start early to prepare for work.

Table 1.3 The Dreyfus Model of Skills Acquisition

	Knowledge	Standard of work	Autonomy	Coping with complexity	Perception of context
1. Novice	Minimal or 'textbook' knowledge without connecting it to practice	Unlikely to be satisfactory unless closely supervised	Needs close supervision or instruction	Little or no conception of dealing with complexity	Tends to see actions in isolation
2. Beginner	Working knowledge of key aspects of practice	Straightforward tasks likely to be completed to an acceptable standard	Able to achieve some steps using own judgement, but supervision needed for overall task	Appreciates complex situations but only able to achieve partial resolution	Sees actions as a series of steps
3. Competent	Good working and background knowledge of area of practice	Fit for purpose, though may lack refinement	Able to achieve most tasks using own judgement	Copes with complex situations through deliberate analysis and planning	Sees actions at least partly in terms of longer-term goals
4. Proficient	Depth of understanding of discipline and area of practice	Fully acceptable standard achieved routinely	Able to take full responsibility for own work (and that of others where applicable)	Deals with complex situations holistically, decision-making more confident	Sees overall 'picture' and how individual actions fit within it
5. Expert	Authoritative knowledge of discipline and deep tacit understanding across area of practice	Excellence achieved with relative ease	Able to take responsibility for going beyond existing standards and creating own interpretations	Holistic grasp of complex situations, moves between intuitive and analytical approaches with ease	Sees overall 'picture' and alternative approaches; vision of what may be possible

Source: Lester, 2005.

Firstly, preparing for work is not about acquiring facts about the workplace. It is about *experientially* developing a tacit and intuitive understanding about work and gradually learning how to adapt effectively to the workplace. Such internalization takes a long gestation time in order to form a person's work persona or identity of the profession. It can only take place by being immersed in the social environment and experiencing the daily happenings in the workplace. The learning is in the participation in work activities, in the building of social relationships and adapting to the norms and culture to become a member of the working community (Lave & Wenger, 1991).

The second reason is that when students get acquainted with the workplace, their learning in school becomes purposeful. They will begin to see how the learning in school fits into the real world, what to focus on, and what projects to embark on. Ultimately it leads towards more outcome-based and self-directed learning. This is often seen in the learning behaviour of working adult students. They may not excel in articulation of theories but they learn deliberately so as to apply the theories in their workplace.

As mentioned before, the knowledge gained in the workplace is multidimensional. Learning to work well in the workplace requires many personal effectiveness and social skills such as communication skills, project management skill, and handling peers and superiors. There is a difference in practising social and communicative skills with fellow students and practising it in a work setting. In this respect, learning to work well in the workplace also helps to nurture character and personal development which are key prerequisites for greater success in one's life.

Preparing for Work While in School

Acknowledging that it is beneficial to prepare for work early, how should students go about doing so while in school? Many would doubt whether it is feasible as they are already so busy catching up with schoolwork, leaving them no time to learn about work.

Preparing for work in school does not necessarily mean spending more time or doing extra work. What is needed, however, is a shift in one's attitude regarding education and work as well as recognising the need to manage one's own career.

First and foremost, students should start taking personal ownership of developing their careers. They should start asking themselves what they have to do now to ensure that they thrive in the VUCA world. More specifically, they must have a clear idea of how to develop their career pathways. As the famous management guru Peter Drucker once said, we have to be our own Chief Executive Officer. It is up to us to carve out our place and adapt ourselves in the constantly changing working world.

Developing a career requires a clear strategy. Students have to be clear about their own career choices and the reasons for a particular career. The choice should be based on the matching of one's interest and passion rather than on salary, prestige or expectation from parents. Recognising the importance of early career counselling, one of the key recommendation of ASPIRE is to provide more education and career guidance (ECG) in schools. With this in place, students can approach the ECG counsellors easily.

Once students are clear about their career choices, they should start finding out more about the industry related to their careers. Preparing for work ultimately boils down to developing the identity of the profession and knowing the real work practices in order to be able to make a contribution to the prospective employer. It also means getting more exposure outside school by establishing direct or indirect contacts with the industry or workplace. There are also many resources and tools available in schools that students can tap on to practise their knowledge. However, to rely on schools to provide every aspect of career development is not realistic as every one's need is different. There is no one size that fits all.

There are various possibilities listed below that aspiring professionals can undertake to prepare early for work.

1. Getting to know the industry well

Keeping informed about the trends and issues of industry is important. There are various trade magazines and online industry portals that provide information about industry reports, technology, market scans and the happenings in the industry or economy as a whole. It is worthwhile to keep current about happenings in the industry. Not only does it create a positive impression on prospective employers but it also provides a useful background for easier assimilation in the workplace later.

2. Professional societies

Professional societies such as the Institute of Electrical and Electronics Engineers (IEEE) or Certified Public Accountants (CPA) Society often provide student membership and good opportunities for professionals to keep current in the profession. While students may not fully appreciate or understand many of the issues discussed, it certainly helps to create awareness of topics that are in the key agenda of the profession. Professional societies also offer many information dissemination opportunities through seminars and networking events. There are possibilities to solicit advice from practitioners via networking. Such opportunities are invaluable in providing informal guidance on career and work. The importance of networking is highlighted in Chapter 11 of this book.

3. Opportunities to meet industry players

Industry seminars, trade fairs and exhibitions are excellent platforms for networking and gathering of information about the industry and workplace. Many schools often offer students opportunities to attend such events. By talking to various people and professionals one can get a fairly good view about the new technology, suppliers and the industry ecosystems and at the same time, helps to build self-confidence in relating to people in the industry.

4. Direct engagement with industry and companies

Direct engagement with industry allows for intensive learning about work. This can be in the form of internships, industrial attachments or student project work with the industry. All these engagements allow students to get a direct experience about work. It is important to demonstrate excellent performance in these engagements as this may lead to future employment opportunities with the company.

One of the key recommendations under ASPIRE vis-à-vis SkillsFuture is for a more structured and longer internship in the industry. Internship is only valuable if students come with the correct learning attitude and are fully engaged in participating in work practices. Not only do students have the opportunity to practise their knowledge and skills but more importantly, students are also able to develop social competencies in terms of relating to different people while immersing in the workplace culture. The enculturation process leads to a sharpened awareness and acuity of the social cultural environment of the workplace.

Where possible, students should solicit project work with the industry rather than getting a topic from school for their project work. Through the industry case study, students will have a chance to understand the work practices better — not only in terms of the task itself but also the tools, methodology and the thinking associated with real work. Real-life case studies allow students to make a direct contribution to the workplace.

5. From holistic to T-shaped development

While students are exposed to a holistic education for a good part of their educational life, the training of a professional requires a more focused approach. Development of a profession normally takes a T-shaped approach, that is, by developing a core set of skills required for the profession in depth and supplemented by set of social and personal competencies (refer to Chapters 3–7) and skills required for effective job performance in the profession. This is encapsulated in most of professional competency standards. Using the competency standards as a guide, students will understand the key requirements for the profession. They can then plan and direct their own learning journey by focusing on core and supplementary skills they need to develop and practise. Whenever possible, they should integrate these competencies into their projects and practise them.

6. Developing the work persona of a professional

Learning to be a professional is not simply about acquiring skills and knowledge only; rather, it encompasses "appropriating" many aspects embodied in a profession such as ethics and values, worldview, and reading, evaluating and handling situations. It is about developing the "being" of a professional. Such understanding is best learned traditionally through a master-apprentice or in the modern-day context of a "mentor-mentee" relationship. For example, a novice chef learning under a master chef not only learns the technique of preparing the food but also the whole works of a chef embodied and expressed through the being of the master chef.

In this respect, finding a good mentor and role model will greatly enhance the student's professional development, especially during his or her internship or early career. Such a mentor-mentee relationship is invaluable in helping to facilitate learning and exposure within the company. A mentor does not necessarily have to be determined by the company. Students can always look for someone knowledgeable in the company whom they are comfortable with to be their mentors. People are often flattered and are willing to offer advice when one asked to be a mentor.

7. Developing personal and social skills

A key part of learning for work and by work is learning how to make an effective contribution in the workplace. Unlike in school, learning in the workplace requires a learning approach that is reflective, participatory as well as communicative. It involves learning to connect all aspects of professional practice. Through this process students learn to develop a more holistic situational awareness of the organisation.

As mentioned earlier, learning in the workplace is also unstructured and informal. People learn in the workplace by immersion and participation in the workplace activities as they encounter different situations to resolve problems. To learn successfully in the workplace requires one to be open and willing to manage oneself. Learning to relate and communicate with others is important. Therefore, in the workplace, both emotional quotient (EQ) and adversity quotient (AQ) are more important than intelligent quotient (IQ). It is only by engaging in conversations and relating with different age groups, departments, or hierarchies that students can gradually develop their emotional maturity.

In conclusion, in the 21st century, more is demanded from our younger generation to be work-ready. This calls for not only knowledge and skills but also for personal and social competencies for workplace practices (Chapters 3–7). There should not be a separation between learning in school and learning at work. They are part of a continuum of one's lifelong learning to cope with, and adapt to, the changing circumstances of one's life and society in general.

Preparing for work benefits young people as they embark on their career journey. Not only are they preparing for a vocation but at the same time, they are also preparing for their life journey. The key is to take ownership for their own development, to be the best they can be and thereby making a meaningful contribution to society. Success will follow.

References

Devin, B. (1998). Sense-making theory and practice: An overview of user interests in knowledge seeking and use. *Journal of Knowledge Management*, 2(2), 36–46.

Eraut, M., Maillardet, F., Miller, C., Steadman, S., Ali, A., Blackman, C., Caballero, C., & Furner, J. (2005). What is learned in the workplace and how? Typologies and results from a cross-professional longitudinal study. Early Career Learning in the Professional Workplace, EARLI Conference, Cyprus.

Eraut, M., Wisker, G., & Barlow, J. (2007). Making teaching more effective. Articles from the Learning and Teaching Conference, University of Brighton Press Centre for Learning and Teaching.

Imel, S. (2000). *Contexual Learning in Adult Education*. Practice Application Brief No 2. ERIC Clearinghouse on Adult, Career and Vocational Education, Ohio State University, Columbus OH. Retrieved from http://files.eric. ed.gov/fulltext/ED448304.pdf

Lave, J. & Wenger, E. (1991). *Situated Learning: Legitimate Peripheral Participation*. Cambridge, England: University of Cambridge Press.

Lester, S. (2005). *Novice to Expert: The Dreyfus Model of Skill Acquisition*. Stan Lester Development. Retrieved from http://www.sld.demon.co.uk/ dreyfus.pdf

Ministry of Education Singapore (August 2014). Applied Study in Polytechnics and ITE Review (ASPIRE) Report.

National Science Board (2014). *Science and Engineering Indicators 2006*, NSB 04-01B. Retrieved from http://www.nsf.gov/statistics/seind14/index. cfm/overview

The Economist (5 October 2006). *The Search for Talent*. Retreived from http:// www.economist.com/node/8000879

Trow, W. (2000). From mass higher education to universal access, The American Advantage Research and Occasional Papers Series. Center for Studies in Higher Education, University of California, Berkeley.

Weick, K. (1995). *Sensemaking in Organizations*. Thousand Oaks, CA: SAGE Publications, Inc.

Chapter 2

Why Youths Need to Be Prepared for Work

Eden Liew

In Singapore, most youths will spend 10 to 12 years in general on school education which includes primary, secondary and, if applicable, junior college education. This is followed by two or more years on professional or vocational education in tertiary institutions which include universities, polytechnics and institutes of technical education (ITEs).

In the case of ITE, secondary school students seeking admission have a wide range of choices. There are over 100 courses in ITE, ranging from "hard" technical subjects to others such as business, hospitality, design and healthcare. Most of the courses are done over two years. The five polytechnics in Singapore similarly have hundreds of diploma-level courses lasting three years. All these programmes are "terminal qualifications" so that graduates upon leaving the institutions can go directly to work without further training. Together with local universities, these post-secondary institutions ensure Singapore has the relevant human resources needed for industry development. The number of training places are planned carefully, and generously funded, based on projected manpower needs for the nation. In fact, most graduates from our institutions are able to find relevant employment upon graduation.

To meet employers' needs, ITEs and polytechnics are regularly in touch with various industries on the development of new programmes, and constantly reviewing their courses so that training stays relevant to industry needs. We engage industry experts to analyse the actual training needs when preparing new programmes. In ITE, this is done under the well-established DACUM (Developing a Curriculum) process. We also set up many advisory committees for industry leaders to work with our academics for reviewing new and existing curriculums. At the highest governance level of each institution, there are always several industries, unions and government representatives providing input for the directions of the institution.

All ITE and polytechnic staff have several years of relevant industry experience and can guide students on the real practices as well as provide the theoretical foundation. There are many schemes for staff to be updated regularly even in academia, e.g., through industry attachment and by involvement in real industry projects. In certain instances, current industry practitioners are also engaged part-time to provide training relevant to specific needs. The laboratories and training facilities are equipped with some of the latest facilities available in the industry as provided by the generous government budget for education — and in particular, vocational education. Another important source for regular equipment upgrading in our laboratories and centres, is through the very close partnerships with major industrial players. Many of such partners see the importance of working closely with educators to ensure our students are trained with the latest systems offered within their industry. In ITEs and polytechnics, we receive many foreign education delegates and bring them around our facilities. Inevitably, many would comment favourably on the training facilities.

While students can have access to the best programmes, teachers and physical facilities, it is also important that they are exposed to the real work environment through industry attachments and internships. Not only will interns be exposed to real production facilities and systems, they will also understand the other requirements needed in all jobs — including soft skills e.g., good team work, project management and communications. In fact, many employers find soft skills more important than technical knowledge as students can be easily trained on the job. ITE and polytechnic lecturers often note that after industrial attachment, students are more mature and motivated, having worked side by side with adult workers.

In recent years, the Singapore government has taken further efforts to develop deep vocational skills in Singaporeans, and integrate learning with practice. This important governmental effort was highlighted in the recommendations of the Applied Study in Polytechnic and ITE Review (ASPIRE) Committee headed by Senior Minister of State Ms Indranee Rajah. Some of the key recommendations include helping students in making better career choices e.g., through better counselling services in schools and institutions, acquiring deeper skills by having employers involved through more industrial attachment and internship schemes, and providing more career progression pathways supported by sector-specific skill frameworks. There is further development to integrate education, training and career, with the setting up of a tripartite SkillsFuture Council headed by Deputy Prime Minister Tharman Shanmugaratnam.

Why is there such an emphasis on formal education? Below are four important reasons amongst others, why youths today should make the best of their formal education to prepare themselves for their future in today's workplace.

Changing Work Environment

The world is changing rapidly today. The workplace is transforming too. In the past, youths started working at a very young age, unlike today's youth. They would work in areas like farming, trade or services. Most would gain their skills by learning from older workers on the job through apprenticeship. In those days, such training was enough for a lifetime. Most workers continue on the same job, and often, with the same employer till retirement. The activities in the workplace then changed very slowly, or might not change at all.

Today's jobs are different. The tempo of change is faster now and will be even more so in the future. A machinist retiring today would, at the start of his career, have been working with, and specialising in, one or two pieces of equipment which required constant attention and adjustment. Today, with advanced computer numerical controlled (CNC) machines, the same job can be completed with minimal human intervention, and the same technician may be working concurrently on several machines at a time. Each of these expensive machines can do the work of several machines in the past and would require greater understanding of the processes. Hence, during a machinist's single working life of just over a few decades, the trade has transformed significantly.

These changes are also reflected in other non-engineering industries. For example, in banking, the traditional bank teller jobs were taken over by ATMs, to the convenience and delight of consumers. On the other hand, the bank staff at the counter now must offer a wide variety of banking transactions in addition to the traditional teller duties for customers who refuse to use ATMs. To cope with this change, counter staff are better qualified, and may even have university qualifications. Preparing for work is now more important than ever to enable a person to cope with complex work situations.

Another aspect of this change is that a person may move through many jobs in the modern economy. In traditional societies, many workers stayed in a single job and with perhaps a similar employer all their lives. Today, economies evolve quickly. New companies and industries are started, while old ones are eliminated. The affected workers would have to move on. This is what some economists term "creative destruction". This pace is even faster in the developed nations as many industries moved to countries with lower labour cost. In Singapore, we started our industrialisation with emphasis on textile and heavy industries. These have disappeared. Even high technical industries were not spared. Singapore used to produce the largest number of hard disk drives for the world market, and this industry has also vanished locally. Due to such changes, workers are forced to find new jobs and in newer industries. In the United States, it is estimated that workers change jobs more than 11 times in their lifetime. Hence, today's youths must stay thoroughly relevant in the workplace and continously upgrade themselves. The employers' corresponding demands are higher. In the past a secondary education was sufficient for a respectable career. Today, most teaching positions will require a university degree. Similarly, businesses are complex organisations requiring staff trained for operational, finance and human resource roles. In addition, staff must be equipped to face a changing commercial environment. In short, any job entrant in most businesses must be better qualified and continue to be an independent and self-regulated learner. This will require a very strong and broad curriculum foundation developed in school.

Advances in Technology

Today, the world is driven by technology. An example is the prevalent use of infocomm technology (ICT) in all parts of Singapore and the world. In fact, Prime Minister Lee Hsien Loong recently announced the "Smart Nation" initiatives. The ICT revolution has also changed the workplace in the last few decades — be it in the manufacturing or services sectors. It is everywhere e.g., smart mobile devices for communication, gaming, and even work. The ICT revolution is now sweeping common equipment such as watches, cars and television sets. This will get even more pervasive as we move towards the Internet of Things (IoT) — when more equipment will be embedded with electronic intelligence and communications capabilities. Another great technological advance is in the bioscience areas which help improve health and nutrition of humans. A deep understanding of all these revolutionary changes will help workers as more companies get involved in different aspects of such development. Even from the perspective of the consumers, a good appreciation of the basics is needed to take advantage of these changes.

It is crucial that youths should use their time in school studying mathematics, science and technology. This is to enable them to understand the environment which is dependent on the application of such new knowledge. It is relatively easy to appreciate general subjects such as literature and history outside school — by reading widely, or even through distance learning. For the hard sciences and mathematics, discipline is needed to systematically help students progress from the fundamentals before advancing to more complex topics. Such learning can only be achieved in a structured curriculum. The laboratories and workshops available in educational institutions also help learners to appreciate the practical aspects.

Importance of Soft Skills

When employers are asked about preparation for new school leavers entering the job market, the most frequent response is the requirement for "soft skills" in the workplace. Many would note that specific job knowledge can be acquired in the workplace, while soft skills cut across all industries and take longer time to develop. Soft skills include communication, problem solving and teamwork. Some of such skills are taught in classrooms in subjects such as General Paper, World Issues and Life Skills. However, more often, such skills need practice, and can be better acquired outside classrooms or lecture theatres. Some activities in developing soft skills include publishing newsletters, engaging in debates and forums, going for outdoor adventures, playing team sports, working on community events or participating in overseas trips.

Unfortunately, many students are focused on doing well academically, getting as many As in class or scoring the perfect grade point average (GPA). In fact, the years spent in school are excellent opportunities to develop soft skills outside curriculum time. Schools provide the safest environment for a person to test some of these skills. The cycles of experimentation, regardless of successes or failures, are great training opportunities for young adults. They can be done without fear of being ridiculed since everyone is in the process of learning, and learning from each other. The experience gained in school will be useful for a lifetime. In contrast, the workplace is more competitive and brutal. Mistakes are not easily tolerated. Adult workers may no longer have the opportunities available that are found in the safe environment of school or under the guidance of nurturing teachers.

Hobbies and Interests

While it is important to help prepare youths for the workplace, there are other important life issues to consider using the time available in schools. One important aspect is preparing for healthy recreation interests outside work — and even in the longer term, retirement after work. Schools, ITEs, polytechnics and universities are large communities of individuals with diverse and varied interests. It is a rare chance for one to be amongst hundreds and even thousands of friends in a similar age group. An example is rugby. It takes 15 or more students to form a team for regular practice and training. That's not all. To have more fun, it is necessary to play competitively in a good tournament, and there is a need to find a few more groups of 15 players who have similarly trained as hard and be prepared for the bruises and injuries in the field. There are also the coaches, referees, linesmen and supporters with their drums and clappers. There must be hundreds of interested individuals to make such games successful. After leaving school, such opportunities cease to exist as most work organisations do not have the people or time for activities such as rugby. The only exceptions are large organisations such as the army and enforcement services which also have emphasis on fitness. Of course, rugby is perhaps a special case where the number of adult players are very limited — at least in Singapore. Healthy recreational activities such as badminton, basketball and football can be acquired during school days and continued long after graduation. Youths can take advantage of fellow students with similar interests, and can enjoy playing with other players with the same level of competencies instead of struggling with expert players, or with novices on the other hand. Moreover, many schools do own the necessary sports infrastructure and also provide coaches to assist in developing further skills. With the confidence gained in schools, a working graduate with meaningful involvement in recreational activities may be able to keep a healthy life regime. Similarly, this applies to the areas of culture and arts, community services, outdoor adventures and other recreational interests.

Most adults pick up such interests during their formative years in school and continue such recreational activities over a lifetime. As mentioned in the previous section, these are also excellent opportunities for the training in soft skills, such as leadership, teamwork, problem solving and project management. It would be a wasted opportunity for students to focus entirely on academic achievements by not being involved in the many co-curricular activities (CCA) available in schools and institutions. There is another aspect to the importance of CCA participation. While tertiary institutions are to train students for their professions or vocations, some graduates are diverted to their interest through CCA. In ITE, many soccer players join professional clubs, and launch their sporting career while in college — the most famous example being Fandi Ahmad. Others move into careers in the arts and culture, having discovered their talents in singing, dance, drama or the visual arts. They use school as a platform to hone their public performance skills and even build a following. Some have gone into non-traditional careers such as being trainers in adventure learning. This might appear a "waste" of the original vocation training. However, it is important that youths discover their real passion in school and develop a lifelong career based on their interests. Institutions are often constrained by the selection of interesting programmes and limited training places within each programme. Very often students are placed in programmes based on their previous academic grades other than their real interests. Nevertheless, the formal training processes in any discipline would also be beneficial when applied to other vocations. For example, technical training in ICT could be relevant to a graduate who decides to pursue sports or entrepreneurship.

Given the above reasons, it is important that youths make the best of Singapore's much admired education system. They should complete their basic primary/secondary education and then pursue vocational or professional training to be ready for the workplace. They must be committed to this strategy to survive in the future. Unfortunately, there are some students who discontinue education and start work early. Some find that there is no reason to study when they were able to earn "sufficient" income doing part-time work while in school. Some students feel that they can discontinue studies and progress to full-time work after having gained some experience in part-time jobs. This is especially common for students who work in hospitality and retail industries which are constantly short of workers. Many of these jobs require minimal skills preparation. Unfortunately, such workers are always competing with the next generation of part-time youths or fresh job entrants. In such cases, the salary will always be pegged close to a fresh, youthful, job entrant or part-time worker. Typically, inexperienced youths doing a part-time job can ask for low wages as they normally live with their parents and have no responsibilities other than personal expenses.

On the other hand, as youths grow into adulthood, they need to advance in their career for better salaries and prospects. This is necessary as they take on heavier life responsibilities such as raising a family and owning a home. To progress further, they need to have deep knowledge of the industry. For example, in a petrochemical plant with very expensive infrastructural investment, the workers must be familiar with the operations of complex systems and components. This familiarity can be achieved through strong fundamentals in technology and the sciences, followed by years of experience working in the field. Workers must have the resourcefulness to deal with trickier problems and the functional literacies to explain their solution to their customers. Such workers are paid well above the typical inexperienced job entrants. This can be achieved only if individuals persist in their education and discover their passion and interest before pursuing their career. It is hoped that all youths will take lifelong learning seriously as it is very important for their future.

Part 2

Developing Social-Emotional Competencies for Life

Chapter 3

Understanding Oneself
through Self-Awareness

Jessie Ee

Introduction

In this rapidly changing globalised landscape, how adequate are we in preparing ourselves for the unknown future ahead of us so that we can be confident, self-directed, concerned citizens and active contributors for tomorrow's world? Are we conscious of our strengths, interests, values and beliefs to equip ourselves with the right knowledge, skills and attitudes to mould the next generation as we become employees, parents and worthy individuals in the community? How important is developing our awareness of ourselves so that we will have a more accurate self-perception and thereby be able to match our strengths with the right career choices we make?

What is Self-Awareness?

Self-awareness includes skills in recognising one's own emotions and cultivating one's strengths and positive qualities. It includes a *realistic* assessment of one's own abilities and a well-grounded sense of self-confidence. This first level is representative of the individual self and revolves around the level of knowing, that is, acquiring knowledge, within the parameters of facts and concepts. At this level, the individual may be able to distinguish right from wrong. However, these are only factual knowledge and we have yet to demonstrate through our actions which are still very much controlled and shaped by our innate abilities (e.g., feelings, emotions, thinking), environment and upbringing.

Considering our innate abilities, how aware are we of our physical body cues e.g., when our hands are cold, our knuckles are white and our stomach gets all knotty? Does it alert us that we are scared of something and if so, what must we do to overcome these body cues? Does it indicate that we must relax? How aware are we?

Or when we are asked to make an oral presentation of our project to our lecturers or our clients or employers, and we develop cold feet, our hands seem wet and cold, we stutter or are lost for words — do these body cues prompt us again that we may not be prepared in our content knowledge or that we lack confidence or we are having an anxiety attack? Does it indicate that we must learn to relax and take control of ourselves? How conscious or aware are we about the signals from our body?

Sometimes, we are tired after completing our assignments or we have had a bad day at work and an innocent comment from someone triggers anger in us. We develop hot flushes, our faces turn red and we feel all hot; we are likely to say things that we may subsequently regret. Are we conscious of what triggers our anger? If we are aware of the signs from our body, we can take control of ourselves. Listen to your inner voice. We can use positive self-talk e.g., "He said that I can't do it. I believe I can do it." It is important to realise that you do not want that anger to take control of you. There is a need to recognise the negative voice e.g., "He said that I can't do it. I must be a failure" and substitute it with something positive so that the negative remarks do not undermine us e.g., "I am even more determined to show them that I can do it. I will strategise and improve myself." Are we conscious if we are more inclined to positive or negative thoughts and are not able to regulate our thoughts in a positive way?

If we recognise our strengths and areas that may need improvement, we can capitalise on our strengths and identify our career path well so that we fit in our workplace. We can further learn to use our strengths to compensate for our areas of weakness and be proactive to learn from our mentors on the job to reduce our limitations. Furthermore, in the workplace, we need to be aware of what our employers, co-workers, clients and subordinates expect of us. If our boss likes facts, when you meet him do ensure that you have done your research so that you can justify what you have to say. Also, be conscious that employers like their employees to solve the problem and not pose problems with lots of questions. What upsets employers when they assign a task is to hear the employee saying, "I can't do it." It is preferable to say "I will try" or "I see what I can do."

What do We Need to be Self-Aware?

If we understand our personality, values, expectations and beliefs, we may realise how compatible we are in the career that we are pursuing or the life partner that we have chosen. Take time to reflect on the questions below and strive to answer them to have a better understanding of yourself.

What do you know about yourself?

- your understanding of respect, relationships and reconciliation
- your values, beliefs and culture
- your expectations — e.g., of yourself, your family members, your colleagues
- your environment — e.g., your workplace, home, social circle
- your task demands and your clients
- your relationships with your family members, colleagues and others

What do you **need to know** about yourself?

- What triggers your anger?
- What are your strengths?
- What are your weaknesses?
- What values do you possess?
- What drives you?
- What are your prejudices/emotional bias?
- How can you be conscious of consistently engaging in ethical, safe and legal ways?

Advantages of Self-Awareness

The more self-aware we are, the more confident we will be of ourselves. This is because through greater exposure, our experience widens and we are likely to be more accepting of others and open to new experiences. This self-awareness will also assist us to be more accurate in assessing others. Thus, we are better at setting more realistic goals and achieving them and are more likely to have a better positive view of ourselves. Indirectly, with greater self-awareness and experience, we are also able to develop better self-confidence of ourselves which in turn leads to greater success in life.

If we are preparing to work in the near future are we aware of the current job trends? Are we aware of what our employers demand? Van Velsor and Wright (2012) conducted an online global survey of 462 respondents (57% males and 43% females) who held managerial roles in the business, government, non-profit and education sectors of which 72% are from United States. Table 3.1 shows the results of this survey, comparing employers' expectations 20 years ago with their expectations today as well as for the near future. Employers felt that the young generation lacks critical soft skills e.g., communication, collaboration, creativity and critical thinking. More than 54% of respondents rank leadership or executive-level skills as the number one soft skill gap. Furthermore, the five top competencies that employers look for in today's workforce are self-motivation and discipline, effective communication, learning agility, self-awareness and adaptability in their

Table 3.1 Comparison of Respondents' View of Employees' Needed Competencies

20 Years Ago		Today		10 Years from Now	
Technical Mastery	53%	Self-motivation/ Discipline	44%	Adaptability/ Versatility	29%
Self-motivation/ Discipline	46%	Effective communication	40%	Effective communication	26%
Confidence	32%	Learning agility	29%	Learning agility	24%
Effective communication	31%	Self-awareness	26%	Multicultural awareness	22%
Resourcefulness	20%	Adaptability/ Versatility	22%	Self-motivation/ Discipline	20%
		Collaboration	20%		

employees. Employers also appreciate young employees' comfort with technology and social networks for information and connectivity, and their creativity, openness and fresh ideas, and multicultural and global awareness. In today's global economy where companies have the option to relocate their businesses anywhere in the world, the workforce needs to be more adaptable, agile and flexible in their thinking and have greater multicultural awareness as they need to be able to communicate effectively and collaborate with different nationalities.

According to Van Velsor and Wright (2012), respondents are most concerned about the next generation of youths for the following reasons:

- They have an unjustified or unrealistic sense of entitlement, and a need for instant gratification and affirmation.
- They lack the ability to communicate face-to-face and are over-dependent on technology.
- They lack a strong work ethic, focus, commitment, drive and self-motivation.
- They lack learning opportunities (e.g., mentoring, positive role models and training) adequate for the future challenges they will face.
- They need decision-making skills, long-term perspective and the ability to understand complexity.
- They lack a strong sense of values, ethics and social responsibility.
- They lack reflection, self-awareness and maturity.
- They are overconfident and not open to input or feedback — their view is the only view.

Much of the employers' concerns are about employees' values, and their lack of social emotional competencies (e.g., lack of self-awareness, social awareness, self-management, relationship management and responsible decision making) and confidence level. Being aware of the employers' concern regarding our limitations, we may need to act on them and attempt to improve in these areas. Being aware of our own strengths and limitations, we can be more competent in setting relevant and realistic goals to ensure that we will not fall short of the demands and expectations of our future employers and be better prepared for tomorrow. We must be mindful that a major blind spot is the lack of clear career goals.

Setting Goals

Goal setting helps us to focus our effort in achieving what we set out to do without being distracted. Indirectly, it helps us to organise our time and resources more effectively in anticipation of the objective we set.

The first step in setting goals is to consider what we want to achieve whether it is short-term goals or long-term goals. Our goals may be related to improving ourselves or others and may relate to our career (e.g., to be a principal in five years' time), attitude (e.g., to develop better self-control), family (e.g., how to be a good parent), financial situation (e.g., to shop for what I need and not for what I desire) or physique (e.g., to slim down).

Goals are often not achieved if we are not aware that we have conflicting goals (e.g., we want to slim down but we enjoy good food) or if we plan poorly and do not monitor or regulate our goals.

A useful way of making effective and achievable goals is to plan and use the SMART mnemonic. SMART stands for Specific, Measurable, Attainable, Relevant and Timely.

- S — Specific goals tend to answer the six "W" questions:

*Who: Who is involved?
*What: What do I want to accomplish?
*Where: Identify a location.
*When: Establish a time frame.
*Which: Identify requirements and constraints.
*Why: Specific reasons, purpose or benefits of accomplishing the goal.

Example: if the general goal is "to improve my communication skills", then the specific goal would be "to improve my communication skills **by practising an hour daily with my best friend so that I can communicate fluently and be successful in an interview in a month's time with 80% success**".

- M — Measurable goals: establishing concrete criteria e.g., How much? How many? How will I know when it is accomplished?

Example: "to improve my communication skills **by interacting with at least two tourists and being evaluated by them with 80% success rate**".

This is to ensure that one is not nervous and is at ease to answer any probing questions from strangers.

- **A** — Attainable: to ensure that the goal is achievable and practical to attain.

Example: "to improve my communication skills **by practising an hour daily** with my best friend for one month".

- **R** — Realistic: to ensure that you are both willing and able to achieve the goal and make substantial progress with available resources, knowledge and time.

Example: "to improve my communication skills **by making PBL presentations and doing interviews with my best friend and team members**".

- **T** — Timely: goals should be grounded within a time frame.

Example: "to improve my communication skills by selling myself during an interview with 80% success rate **in a month's time**".

Awareness of Your Life Purpose

Life becomes meaningful only when a person is driven by a high goal that is guiding him or her. It is important to be able to see the vision at the end of the tunnel. A sense of purpose provides the undying passion and steadfast commitment to do what you need to do. It gives you worthy goals to strive for. If you are lacking in self-awareness, reflect on your strengths and interests and those whom you highly respect and wish to model after.

Reference

Van Velsor, E. & Wright, J. (2012). *Expanding the Leadership Equation: Developing Next-Generation Leaders*. Center for Creative Leadership, White Paper. Retrieved on 7 February 2015 from http://www.ccl.org/Leadership/pdf/research/Expanding LeadershipEquation.pdf

Activity: Knowing Your Strengths and Areas for Improvement

Use the following assessment tools to identify your strengths and areas for improvement:

1. Social Emotional Learning Questionnaire (SELQ)
   http://eejessie.blogspot.sg/p/blog-page.html

2. Personality Questionnaire
   http://psychologytoday.tests.psychtests.com/bin/transfer?req=
   MTF8MTI5N3w1Njg1NjY2fDF8MQ==&refempt=
   or
   http://www.16personalities.com/

3. Learning Style
   http://www.edutopia.org/multiple-intelligences-learning-styles-quiz

4. Self-esteem
   http://www.wwnorton.com/college/psych/psychsci/media/ rosenberg.htm

Complete the table by listing your strengths and weaknesses in the respective columns. Then, consider ways you intend to use your strengths to overcome your areas of weaknesses.

Questionnaire	Strengths	Weaknesses	Ways You Intend to Overcome Your Weaknesses
SELQ			
Personality			
Learning Style			
Self-Esteem			

Chapter 4

Managing and Regulating Emotions

Jessie Ee

As humans we are emotional beings. It is important to manage our emotions, as how we express our emotions is often seen as a measure of our professionalism at work. The way we express our emotions is also a reflection of our character.

What is Self-Management?

Self-management is the ability to take control of our emotions and being forward-looking, exercising self-control, having flexible thinking, and maintaining composure and positive thinking when confronted with life's challenges. In the process, the ability to regulate our emotions facilitates the task at hand as we pursue our goals, and it encourages perseverance in the face of setbacks and frustrations.

What does Neurobiology have to Say about the Relationship among Our Cognition, Emotions and Behaviour?

Evidence from neurobiological theories indicates that our brain and body have built-in ways to help us self-regulate or manage and control our behaviours. Our sensory input, that is, whatever we see, feel, hear, taste or smell is received by our thalamus which decodes and analyses the input, while the hypothalamus receives signals from the body and is involved in the regulation of drives (e.g., sleep, sexuality, appetite). The thalamus sends the decoded messages to the brain. When we are angry, the thalamus will send them to the amygdala. The primary function of the amygdala is the modulation of neural systems underlying cognitive and social behaviours in response to emotional cues.

Brain research has become yet another field in which scientists argue that social and emotion interactions and functioning are paramount to what is learned. The amygdala will induce our feelings whether pleasant (e.g., happiness) or unpleasant (e.g., fear, anger, sadness or anxiety). If we are angry, the amygdala will induce stress hormones and faster heart beats and send these changes to the cortex which makes us conscious of our anger. The cortex, which is the thinking part of the brain handling memory, perceptual awareness, language and thinking, will interpret the situation. But, because the cortex does not work so fast, we sometimes may say or do something that may cause us to regret it later. However, if we are aware of how our brain and body function, we can develop greater awareness of our feelings and think and reflect before reacting. For example, if we are conscious of our feelings of anger and frustrations, we can tell ourselves "to get a grip". At times, we may need to walk away, rather than deal impulsively with the situation and regret our actions the next minute. Walking away will help us to reflect and control our feelings so that our actions and behaviours will be appropriate.

When powerful emotions (e.g., fear, anger) are experienced under stress, the amygdala imprints this memory with an added degree of strength resulting in emotional charges. Many childhood experiences are emotional charges (e.g., traumatic experiences) and these may have a long-term impact on behaviour. When an association is made with the past experiences, it causes us to re-experience these emotional charges in the present, resulting in a profound effect on current relationships.

How do Our Emotions Affect Our Thoughts and Actions?

According to Mayer *et al.* (2001), emotional and social processes are fundamentally inseparable from cognitive processes. They maintained that emotions help prioritise, decide, anticipate and plan our actions. Zins *et al.*

(2004) found that metacognition is a **good mediator** for enhancing our social emotional competencies as metacognition is thinking about thinking: the more we are aware of our thinking processes as we reflect, the more we can control our goals, dispositions and actions or behaviours. Therefore, as emotions can affect our thoughts and our actions, there is a need to

- recognise and identify our emotions
- understand and take control of our emotions and note the stage we are in
- be conscious of our thinking processes
- ensure that we translate our emotions and thoughts in a positive manner

Our emotions can be either positive feelings (e.g., happiness, excitement, tranquility) or negative feelings (e.g., anger, sadness, pain, denial, panic, anxiety) and these in turn may affect our thoughts and actions. Therefore, we need to be conscious of our emotions and address our thoughts so that our actions will not be negative.

Recognising and Identifying Our Emotions

In order to effectively manage our emotions, we must first learn to accurately recognise and identify them. Some people ignore their emotional reactions e.g., when they lose their spouse or have a break-up. Their denial of their emotions may reflect their lack of self-awareness of this great loss. As such, they may not be able to use their emotions constructively or productively e.g., the one who lost her spouse may be in a state of denial and the one who broke up with her partner may be experiencing "love sickness". Another group may have difficulty regulating their intense emotions e.g., anger, and may not be able to manage their emotions positively resulting even in crimes of passion. Such people have trouble recognising, identifying and managing their emotions.

Besides being aware of our emotions and being able to identify and recognise them, it is also important to take a step back and tell ourselves to "get a grip" of the situation. This will allow us to reflect on the situation and not act impulsively and regret our actions later. However, we must be aware that different people respond in different ways to the same situation because their experiences, cultural backgrounds or levels of self-confidence differ e.g., A confident person may not be upset if her best friend doesn't invite her to a dinner party. She may feel that she also needs her space. But, another person may be offended that her best friend failed to invite her. The way these two people respond to the same situation may be due to their confidence levels, their personalities or their past experiences.

Our body attempts to alert us of our emotions. However, how conscious are we of these physical alerts? When our hands are cold, our knuckles are white and our stomach gets all knotty, does it cue us in that we are scared of something and if so, what must we do to overcome this fear? Does it indicate that we must relax? If so, we could do some deep breathing and relaxation techniques to relax ourselves. We could also take a walk or listen to relaxing music to cool down.

Sometimes, we are tired after a bad day at work and an innocent comment from someone can trigger anger in us. We develop hot flushes and are likely to say things that we may subsequently regret. The inability to handle our emotions may be a measure of our professionalism. Are we conscious of what triggers our anger? If we are aware of our body cues, we can take control of ourselves. Listen to our inner voice. We can use positive self-talk e.g., "He said that I can't do it. I believe I can do it." It is important to realise that you do not want that anger to take control of you. There is a need to recognise the negative voice e.g., "He said that I can't do it. I must be a failure" and substitute it with something positive so that the negative remarks do not undermine us.

How Emotions Reflect Our Actions or Behaviour

In the earlier chapter, we learnt that our knowledge may be shaped by our innate abilities, cultural environment and upbringing e.g. if we are often neglected or assigned to foster homes during our upbringing, we may feel insecure and less likely to trust others.

- Our thoughts and emotions affect our behaviours.
- Positive thoughts often lead to success but they will not work miracles.
- Working hard and accepting responsibilities are essential to success.

How to Take Control of Our Emotions

We are all emotional beings. We may face stressful situations whether at home or in school, the workplace or the community. Negative emotions resulting in bad behaviour may be more tolerated at home and in school, but as adults in the workplace or in the community, such behaviour is less acceptable. In Singapore, a boss was caught on a handphone camera slapping an employee. Due to his lack of emotional control, his company has since closed down. In another situation in India, a millionaire rammed his car into his security guard who was opening the gate too slowly, resulting in the death of the security guard and imprisonment for the millionaire who was accused of murder. The consequences of such displays of rage show that we must be mindful of our emotions.

At work, you may have been working very hard on a project with a colleague only to find your colleague has been laid off and you will have to do his share of the work as well. How do you handle your emotions and manage them productively? If we are focusing on negative emotions, we need strategies to change them into positive emotions. Perceiving the situation positively (e.g.. here's my chance to multi-task and showcase my strengths) will generate feelings of excitement or optimism, resulting in the ability to share our positive emotions constructively and professionally in the workplace. However, if we are not able to think positively or optimistically, we need to do the following:

- Think of a way to calm down by
    — doing something physically active
    — doing something relaxing
    — thinking about something else
    — using centred breathing
    — using positive talk
- Recognise and identify the emotion you are feeling
- Reflect and think of a positive thought and action so that you can get your emotions under control
- Do what is most helpful for yourself and others
- Communicate your emotions clearly to others

What Happens When We have to Make a Decision While We are Experiencing Strong Emotions?

Our minds are powerful. People may forgive our actions but if we don't forgive ourselves, that may be detrimental. Sometimes our minds especially our self-beliefs may be quite obtrusive especially when we have experienced much failure as we are less likely to believe that we can succeed in our performance. If so, we may need to change our thinking:

- Think "I can succeed" and believe you can.
- Affirm and think aloud "I will succeed."
- Believe that you can succeed by setting SMART goals (see Chapter 3) to achieve it.
- Regulate and monitor your progress to fulfil your goal.

It is not your business that everyone around you doesn't think you can succeed. Your business is just to stay focused and strategise and organise your plan so that you can experience the successful outcome.

Alternatively, we may be exposed to daily situations that may frustrate or anger us when our friends disappoint us. For example, you did a joint project with your colleague but your name was left out in the final report. You did all the groundwork and writing so you are understandably upset. How would you address the issue? The following steps are helpful:

1. **IDENTIFY the decision to be made**
   How should I respond to my colleague who has left my name out of the final report?

2. **THINK about your options and reject any that could lead to trouble**
   Possible options:
   1. *Bring it to the boss's notice?*
   2. *Confront my colleague?*
   3. *Arrange a meeting with the boss and my colleague?*
   4. *Spread his wrongdoings to others in the office?*

3. USE QUESTIONS to eliminate negative options and make a responsible decision
   - *Is it against the law, school rules or the teachings of my religion?*
   - *Is it harmful to me or to others?*
   - *Would it disappoint my family or even other important adults?*
   - *Is it wrong to do?*
   - *Would I be hurt or upset if someone did this to me?*

4. PREDICT the consequences of positive options

Option	Advantage	Disadvantage	Rank Options
1. *Bring it to the boss's notice?*	Boss discovers colleague's integrity	Boss may wonder why you didn't speak to colleague first	3
2. *Confront my colleague?*	Matter will be clarified	Break-up in relationship	2
3. *Arrange a meeting with the boss and my colleague?*	Matter will be clarified	—	1
4. *Spread his wrongdoings to others in the office?*	Matter will be clarified	People may think worse of you	4

5. CHOOSE the best choice of action.
   Seek out the advice of an adult who is mature and objective if you are undecided about the options.

6. Rethink the consequences of your actions if the outcome was not well considered.

PUT-DOWNS

INQUIRY: A put-down I once said to someone was:

You are stupid!

ASSUMPTION:
To feel good about myself, I must try to make other people feel bad about themselves.

INVESTIGATING PROCEDURES	PROVEN BELIEF
• Rewrite assumption into a proven belief • Change thoughts • Change behaviours	I don't have to try to make others feel bad about themselves in order to feel good about myself. I have many other better choices.

SELF-TALK

Statements I make to myself that influence me to put down others:
How can he not see the solution!

Statements I make to myself that influence me to build up others:
Maybe he is stressed and failed to see other perspectives!

Help others to feel good!

Maybe we need to consider other perspectives so that we can solve the problem.

ANGER

INQUIRY: A time I got angry was

When someone jumped the queue to catch a taxi

ASSUMPTION:
It is awful, and I must get angry when things don't go the way I want them to go.

INVESTIGATING PROCEDURES	PROVEN BELIEF
• Rewrite assumption into a proven belief • Change thoughts • Change behaviours	Sometimes I would like situations to be different, but I can deal with them calmly or let them go.

SELF-TALK

Statements I make to myself that influence me to get angry:	Statements I make to myself that influence me to want to seek solutions:
How can he jump the queue? He has no right to that taxi as it was not his turn.	Maybe he has more urgent matters to deal with. It is all right as I am in no hurry.

Look for a positive solution!

I can enjoy the scene while waiting for my taxi.

Expressing Our Negative Thoughts and Emotions in Positive Ways

If you are patient in one moment of anger, you will escape a hundred days of sorrow.
~Chinese proverb~

Below are some scenarios that may help us to think and perceive in a positive way. For example, when we perceive someone as taking initiative at work, we may have negative thoughts such as "He must be stupid!" or "He is trying to show off his skills." Maybe we need to perceive it in a positive light and say, "He understands the concept of responsibility." Another negative thinking that we may have is that the person who apologises first after an argument must have been in the wrong. It may not be so — he or she may value the opponent and want to maintain the relationship between them.

Alternatively, you may wish to use "what, why and how" to address your negative thoughts in a more positive manner and change them.

WHAT: Name *what* behaviour is bothering you and *what* you feel.
WHY: Explain *why* this is bothering you.
HOW: Say *how* you would like the other person to behave instead.

Situation: A senior colleague pushes his work to you for you to do.

WHAT: When you (behaviour) _____ I feel _____
WHY: because _____
HOW: I wish (or I want you to) _____

When you <u>assigned this task to me</u>, I feel <u>overwhelmed</u>
because <u>I'm not sure if I can finish the task within a certain time unless
I know the time frame for each task</u>.

I wish <u>you would help me to prioritise as I have a list of tasks assigned by
you to do</u>.

If you articulate your feelings in this way, the senior colleague may realise that he has to take on the task himself if he has to meet certain deadlines, otherwise his boss may know that the task had been delayed because he had assigned the task to someone else.

Some helpful coping strategies for stress and anxiety

Expression of feelings	Express feelings to others through song, poetry, communication, writing or drawing e.g., I tell my dad whom I trust when I feel sad.
Beliefs and values	Believe in God or in someone or something, or in what is right or wrong and in oneself e.g., I believe that I have the ability to solve the problem even though they say that I will fail. Believe in a set of social values e.g., commitment to a task, consideration of others, integrity, care and concern for others, responsibility, empathy.
Cognition	Use rational thinking and learn from past experiences e.g., I think of how I have overcome similar difficulties in the past when I feel disappointed with myself.
Imagination	Use positive and creative ways to solve problems or use the imagination to relax e.g., I think of the rainbow at the end of the road.
Physiology	Engage in physical and relaxation exercises e.g., jogging, walking, swimming, doing exercises, being massaged
Social	Being in the company of others e.g., I have tea and window-shop with my friends when I am sad. Confide in and seek help from mature friends who have objective views.

Websites for Coping with Emotions

Websites on coping with anger

http://www.apa.org/topics/anger/index.aspx
http://www.mayoclinic.com/health/anger-management/MH00102

Websites on coping with depression

http://www.apa.org/topics/depress/index.aspx

Websites on coping with anxiety

http://www.psychologytoday.com/blog/hide-and-seek/201210/coping-anxiety
http://www.anxietybc.com/cbt-video-cbt-skills

Websites on coping with fear

http://www.wikihow.com/Overcome-Fear
http://www.nhs.uk/Conditions/stress-anxiety-depression/Pages/dealing-with-fears.aspx

References

Mayer, J. D., Salovey, P., Caruso, D. R., & Sitarenios, G. (2001). Emotional Intelligence As a Standard Intelligence.*Emotion,* 1(3), 232–242.

Zins, J. E., Bloodworth, M. R., Weissberg R. P., & Walberg H. J. (2004). The scientific base linking social and emotional learning to school success. In Zins, J. E., Weissberg, R. P., Wang, M. C., & Walberg, H.G.(eds.), *Building Academic Success on Social and Emotional Learning: What Does the Research Say?* New York, NY: Teacher's College Press.

Chapter 5

Developing and Promoting Social Awareness

Jessie Ee

What is Social Awareness and Why is it Important?

Social awareness involves the active process of seeking out information about what is happening in the communities around us e.g., recognising what others are thinking and feeling; understanding their emotions, needs and concerns; showing compassion and appreciation; understanding our social norms and problems so that we have a wider perspective and are able to recognise and interact positively with diverse groups.

This is especially important in the global Internet age that we are living in as we are surrounded with various nationalities and need to appreciate diversity. Social awareness skills form the basis for community building. When one feels safe to speak up in an environment that is empathetic, supportive and nurturing, one is more likely to adopt societal norms, respect the rules and apply them. For example, in the home environment, if parents are empathetic, nurturing and supportive and encourage their children to understand others by putting themselves in others' shoes, children may be more likely to exercise perspective taking in seeing their world. Thus, children will be more daring to take on risks and academic challenges and perceive mistakes as a learning process when they are aware that they can turn to adults for support and progress. They can learn more spontaneously to be confident, active and concerned citizens.

Similarly, in the working environment, employees are likely to be motivated to go the extra mile and even take risks if they are able to perceive that their employers are supportive, empathetic and understanding, and appreciate them. Likewise, employees may also need to see from their employers' perspective to understand that they must not procrastinate or provide poor service as these actions can be costly to the organisation. Often we fail to see the bigger picture and judge others superficially.

A teacher was telling her class a story about a ferry that met with a mishap at sea. A couple, in trying to get onto the lifeboat, realised that there was only one space left. The man jumped onto the lifeboat, leaving his wife behind on the sinking ferry. The lady stood on the sinking ferry and shouted one sentence to her husband. The teacher asked the class, "What do you think she shouted?"

Most of the students excitedly answered, "I hate you! I was blind!" The teacher noticed a boy who was silent throughout and asked him what he thought. He replied, "Teacher, I believe she would have shouted — Take care of our child!" The teacher was surprised, asking him, "Have you heard this story before?" The boy shook his head and said, "Nope, but that was what my mum told my dad before she passed away." The teacher sighed, "Your answer is right." The ferry sunk, the man went home and brought up their daughter single-handedly. Many years later after the death of the man, their daughter found his diary while tidying his belongings. It turned out that when her parents took the ferry, the mother had already been diagnosed with a terminal illness. At the critical moment, the father rushed to the only chance of survival. He wrote in his diary, "How I wished to sink to the bottom of the ocean with you, but for the sake of our daughter, I can only let you lie forever below the sea alone." The class was silent at the conclusion of the story. The teacher knew that the students had understood the moral of the story — which is that our perspectives differ because of our emotions and experience. It also highlights the fact that we should not have a narrow perspective. It is important not to focus on the surface and not to judge others without trying to understand them first.

Similarly, on a positive perspective, if someone likes to pay the bill, it may not be because he or she is well-off but that he or she values friendship above money. Or if a person apologises first after a fight, it doesn't mean that the individual is wrong but because he values the people around him. Also, people who are ever willing to help do not help because they feel they owe us anything but because they are truly kind. Finally, we may text someone often, not because we have nothing better to do but because we have them in our hearts.

Failure is often perceived as socially unacceptable but making mistakes is part and parcel of any success journey. Failure should serve as a feedback mechanism for us to improve in the areas that we are weak. In fact, it can be seen as a stepping stone towards success.

Note that there may be multiple perspectives for each scenario. Likewise, the perspective may be positive or negative. If we have been exposed to more experiences through community work, clubs and voluntary organisations, we are more likely to be open to new experiences and be able to see more perspectives. Our positive outlook and our ability to empathise will also widen our circle of friends in school and at work or the community. However, if we restrict ourselves by just going home after work, our perspectives may be narrower because of less exposure to experiences.

How can We Develop Empathy?

The following lists some ways:

- Improve your listening skills.
    — Listen actively to understand the other party's point of view.
    — Take in information without passing judgement.
    — Allow for the expression of emotions and sharing of the problems.
- Pay close attention to others' emotional states.
    — Be aware of changes in body language, facial expressions and tone of voice.
    — Listen carefully to what people say, how they say it and what they do.
    — Notice how they respond to external events such as greetings or requests.

- Reflect on your own feelings.
    - — Ask yourself how the other person's emotions make you feel.
    - — Try to stay objective as you consider different points of view.
- Respond accurately to others' feelings, emotions and moods with non-verbal gestures.
    - — Make positive eye contact.
    - — Lean forward.
    - — Have a relaxed posture.
- Think before you answer.
    - — Keep an open mind and don't judge or interrupt the speaker.
    - — Empathise with the speaker through checking for understanding by paraphrasing or summarising or reviewing.

How can We Nurture Empathy and Mediate for Others?

During conflict resolution (which will be elaborated on in Chapter 6), mediators and disputants need to be able to put themselves in others' shoes if they are to have a wider perspective and be able to empathise, understand and solve conflicts or problems. The following lists the necessary steps:

1. **Introduce yourself to the disputants**
    - — Establish rapport with the disputants and explain to them what the mediation process is all about e.g., "I am Ms X. Both of you seem upset over the issue. Can I assist so that there is a common understanding?"
    - — Ensure that the disputants agree to some ground rules:
        - Do not interrupt.
        - Tell the truth.
        - No name calling or put downs.
        - Work to solve the problem.
2. **Define and explore the problem**
    - — Allow disputants to take turns to give their perspectives of the problem.
    e.g., "Can you tell me what happened?"

— Ask open-ended questions to find out how the disputants are feeling.
e.g., "How do you feel?"

— Assist disputants to see each others' perspectives.
e.g., "How do you feel? How do you think A felt when this happened?"

— Ask more questions to better understand the problem.
e.g., "Is there anything else that you would like to share with me regarding this problem?"

3. **Look for solutions**

— Bring disputants back to the point before the conflict occurred.
e.g., "What could you have done differently?"

— Seek to know how disputants would react if they are given the opportunity to start again in order to prevent the conflict.
e.g., "What can you do right now to help solve the problem?"

— Brainstorm with disputants the possible solutions.
e.g., "Is there anything that needs to be done to help make the solution even better?"

4. **Agree on a solution**

— Check that both disputants are agreeable to the solution proposed.
e.g., "Do you both agree to the solution that you have just indicated that you would be happy with?"

— Ensure that no rules are broken and that no one is physically or emotionally hurt.
e.g., "So are we all agreeable to this solution which is to ...... (describe the solution)?"

— Get both disputants to agree to the time frame to act on the solution.
e.g., "Do we need a time frame to carry out the solutions that we have promised here? If so, when do you think we can get started?"

Developing Social Awareness to Reduce Our Prejudices

Prejudice is groundless and unwarranted. People who are prejudiced tend to have a negative attitude towards members of a group. While specific definitions of prejudice given by social scientists often differ, most agree that it involves prejudgments (usually negative) about members of a group. The types of prejudices may include age, gender, race, nationality, socio-economic status, religion and even sexual orientations.

When prejudice occurs, stereotyping and discrimination may also result. In many cases, prejudices are based upon stereotypes or a simplified assumption about a group. It may be positive (e.g., "old folks are more experienced") or negative (e.g., "old folks are slow"). These stereotypes can lead to faulty beliefs due to prejudice and discrimination.

Some of the causes of prejudice may be fear, ignorance or not liking someone of a different group. There is also the possibility of wanting to feel more powerful than the other group or to keep the status quo. Prejudice may result in more segregation of groups which may be harmful to everyone.

Researchers (e.g., Allport, 1979) have also explored ways to reduce or eliminate prejudice. Training people to become more empathetic to members of other groups is one method that has shown much success. If people are able to imagine themselves in similar situations, they are able to think about how they would react and gain a greater understanding of other people's actions. Indirectly, it is important to create greater social awareness or expressions of empathy so that people can understand and relate to the other groups more positively. Other ways of reducing prejudice include making people aware of anti-prejudice social norms or helping them to be conscious of the inconsistencies of their prejudices. Passing laws and regulations that require fair and equal treatment for all groups of people may be another alternative.

How Conscious are We Regarding Our Prejudices?

The activity below will assist you to assess your prejudices and preferences. You will then be aware of your prejudices and orientations so that your ability to understand others will not be distorted. We should all make a conscious decision to set our prejudices aside and make a conscious effort to minimise their influence on our relationships with others, whether in the home, working environment or community.

Reference

Allport, G. (1979). *The Nature of Prejudice.* Cambridge, MA: Perseus Books.

Activity: What Are Your Prejudices?

Each of us, because of our personal experiences, carries biases and prejudices into our profession. Some of our values, beliefs and assumptions are so ingrained that we are usually unaware of them. Consequently, we will generalise about certain groups of people and create stereotypes. If we trick ourselves into believing these subjective opinions are true facts, we may not be helping ourselves and others.

This quiz is to help you determine your familiarity with, and acceptance of, people who are unlike yourself. Treat the result as a guide to your prejudices.

Give yourself a score as follows:

1. Never 2. Seldom 3. Sometimes 4. Often 5. Always

1. Do you have negative feelings about people from poverty areas?   _____

2. Do you feel girls are not suited for classes like auto mechanics and woodshop?   _____

3. Do you feel uncomfortable when you are surrounded by those who are disabled?   _____

4. Do you dislike males who have "feminine" traits or females who have "masculine" traits?   _____

5. Do you feel that poor people are lazy?   _____

6. Do you tell jokes about disabled individuals?   _____

7. Do you discount opinions of people with low social-economic status?   _____

8. Do you believe girls are less mathematically inclined than boys?   _____

9. Do you feel old folks cannot keep up with the times?   _____

10. Do you get impatient with the disabled because they are so dependent on you and are consistently needing help?   _____

11. Do you dislike assertive females and find them pushy or abrasive?   _____

12. Do you feel old folks are slow in their work?   _____

13. Do you speak negatively of ethnic minorities?   _____

14. Do you feel the values of some poor people are not right?   _____

15. Do you feel that young workers are less experienced?   _____

16. Do you feel that older folks are more conservative in their thinking?   _____

17. Do you avoid taking the time to learn about other's disabilities?   _____

18. Do you dislike the idea of interracial dating or marriage?   _____

19. Do you resent the special opportunities given to ethnic minorities or other nationalities?   _____

20. Do you think it is ever appropriate to imitate certain ethnic groups or nationalities by over-exaggerating their speech patterns or mannerisms?   _____

Add your scores for the statements in the different categories. The total represents your score for each respective prejudice.

Age		Gender		Disabled		Race/Culture		Social-Economic Status	
Question	Score	Question	Score	Question	Score	Question	Score	Question	Score
9		2		3		13		1	
12		4		6		18		5	
15		8		10		19		7	
16		11		17		20		14	
Total		Total		Total		Total		Total	

16–20   You have a biased in this area and need to overcome your prejudices by separating opinions or emotional reactions from the hard truth. Seek a professional who can help you in this process.

9–15   You appear to have some biases but you are somewhat aware of your biases and try to treat people equally whenever possible. Keep plugging away. Continue to expand your knowledge and diversity.

Below 8   You have a few biases and tend to judge most people individually rather than by placing them into generalised groups. Congratulations!

Chapter 6

Relationship Management

Jessie Ee

What is Relationship Management?

Relationship management involves the effective handling of one's emotions in our interactions with others to maintain a healthy and rewarding relationship based on cooperation. The ability to resist inappropriate social pressure and negotiating solutions to conflict or seeking help when needed are other areas in managing relationships. Both affective and cognitive knowledge are important in exercising relationship management in social situations and academic environments. Those who are unable to manage themselves and their relationships might engage in socially inappropriate behaviours and are unlikely to think clearly and perform well academically.

Relationship management plays an important role in leadership, friendship, family life, career life, teamwork, teacher-pupil relationship, parent-child relationship, school-parent relationship and working partnership. Effective and open communication promotes an awareness of others' interests and needs. Being aware of the necessary skills that will encourage open communication is important when working with others.

What are the Obstacles to Harmonious Relationships?

The following is a list of obstacles in establishing good relationships:

1. Prejudice
2. Mistrust
3. Insincerity
4. Lack of integrity
5. Aggression
6. Afraid of losing face
7. "If you are my friend" expectations
8. "I" or "me" mentality
9. Must-win mindset
10. "I am your senior" attitude
11. One-track "individual rights" or "principles"
12. Nepotism and cronyism
13. Taking advantage of others
14. Having wrong values/attributes
15. Putting others down

Gordon (2009) identified 12 communication roadblocks that prevent adults from relating to their children. This may also happen in the office between the employer and the employee and further explains how a breakdown in communication may be obstacles to harmonious relationships. They are:

1. Ordering, directing, commanding

The words may be very authoritarian and may carry a threat of an impending consequence if the advice is not taken.

"This is wrong! You should . . . "
"You've got to face up to reality."
"Stop feeling sorry for yourself!"

2. Warning, threatening

The words sound like threats, with unpleasant consequences if they are not obeyed.

"If you don't study, I will punish you!"
"You're really asking for trouble when you do that."
"You'd better listen to me or you'll be sorry."

3. Moralising, preaching

Using an underlying moral code e.g., using "should" or "ought" to stress proper conduct.

"You should learn. . . "
"You shouldn't do this."
"It's your duty to . . . "

4. Advising, giving solutions

Here the individual draws on his or her own knowledge and experience to recommend a single course of action.

"What I would do is. . . "
"Why don't you. . . "
"Have you tried. . . ?"

5. Persuading with logic

The assumption is that the person has not adequately thought it through and needs help in doing so.

"Here is why you are wrong. . . "
"The facts are that. . . "
"Yes, but. . . "

6. Judging, criticising, blaming

The common element here is the implication that there is something wrong with the person or with what he or she has said. Often the focus is on external sources.

"You are just lazy."
"Maybe you started the fight first. . . "
"It's your own fault."

7. Praising, approving, agreeing

This kind of message gives permission or approval to what has been said and may stop the communication process as it may imply an uneven relationship between the speaker and listener. Likewise, the praising may be for wrong reasons. True listening is different from approving and does not require approval.

"Well, I think you're doing a great job!"
"You're right — your boss is awful."
"I think you are absolutely right."

8. Name calling, shaming, labelling, ridiculing

Here the disapproval is more overt and is directed at the individual in the hope of shaming or correcting a behaviour or attitude.

"Coward!"
"You are always like that!"
"You should be ashamed of yourself."
"That's really stupid."

9. Analysing, diagnosing

It is very tempting for counsellors to seek out the hidden meaning for the person and give their own interpretation.

"What's wrong with you is. . . "
"You're just tired."
"What you really mean is. . . "

10. Reassuring, sympathising

The intent is usually to help the person feel better. But it may be a roadblock because it interferes with the spontaneous flow of communication.

"Don't worry."
"You'll feel better."
"Oh, cheer up!"

11. Questioning, probing

The intent is to probe further. However, it may be perceived that the questioner is rushing to solve the problem and interfering with the flow of the communication. This may come across as being insensitive to the person in question and may prevent further communication.

"Why?"
"Who?"
"What did you. . . ?"

12. Diverting, sarcasm, withdrawal

The intent is to "take the person's mind off it". This will divert communication and implies that what the person was saying is not important or shouldn't be pursued.

"Let's talk about pleasant things. . . "
"Why don't you try running the world?"
Remaining silent, leaving the scene.

What are the Crucial Attributes in Relationships?

The following is a list of attributes/traits or qualities that help to facilitate communication

1. Caring
2. Loyal
3. Honest
4. Trustworthy
5. Sincere
6. Compassionate
7. Empathetic
8. Respectful
9. Kind
10. Faithful

What are Some Ways of Building and Maintaining Healthy Relationships?

Bearing in mind Gordon's 12 communication roadblocks, active listening with discernment must be practised to know what needs to be said and when, so as not to obstruct the communication flow. We have also recognised the importance of empathy so that we are in tune with the speaker. Our awareness of who we are speaking to is also another important criteria e.g., our alertness to the moods of our employers or colleagues, their personalities and what triggers their emotions will assist us in knowing what to say at the right time so that we can relate better with them.

The following exercise may be one way to communicate without offending the listener and getting the message across effectively.

What we can do	How we can do it
Listen to what our friends have to say	Active listening with discernment
Understand and empathise with our friends	Step in, step back, reflect
Tell our friends our feelings	I-message

Practising "I messages"

I feel _____(emotion) when you _____(action)

because_____(reason).

Example

I feel <u>sad</u> when you <u>procrastinate</u> because <u>you could have achieved your goal much earlier.</u>

Ways to Communicate Disagreement with Dignity

The following lists ways in which to communicate disagreement without being emotional:

1. **Calm down** and **think/reflect** before you try to communicate.
2. Use **positive self-talk** to help you think and identify the best perspective for handling the situation successfully.
3. Set a **positive tone** — begin by treating the other person with respect.
4. **Express your point of view.** Use the word "I" not "You".
5. **Listen** to the other person.

Ways to Communicate Assertively and Confidently

What makes others listen and respect what we say? How can we earn the respect and attention of others, e.g., at an interview or when we feel pressurised to succumb to the demands of bullies? We can communicate assertively and confidently by practising the following steps:

1. **Know your facts and have them in hand.** Basically, have the relevant knowledge to support yourself. If you are going for an interview, you may need to know the mission or vision of the organisation, the job scope, the working culture in the organisation and even the likely people who will be interviewing you. If you are encountering a bully, you may need to know the characteristics of bullies (e.g., they lack self-esteem; they lack facts) so that you can counteract them.

2. **Anticipate others' behaviour and prepare your responses.** Visualise what is likely to happen and role-play in your mind — this will increase your confidence and enable you to be assertive. You may wish to prepare other people to support or defend you if you are communicating with a bully.

3. **Prepare good open questions.** This will impress your interviewers that you are interested in their organisation. If you are trying to communicate

with bullies, be aware that they dislike deep, constructive or probing questions. They will be shocked when you display assertiveness and confidence and not succumb to them.

4. **Practise your reactions in the mirror.** This is to check if you have a more confident and assertive manner and are able to appear natural, e.g., no hesitation or stammering or stuttering.

5. **Believe in yourself and have faith that your ability and style will work.**

Ruiz (2000) highlights four important "agreements" for exercising confidence and assertiveness.

1. **Be impeccable with your words.** Speak with integrity. Say only what you mean. Avoid using words to speak against yourself or to gossip about others. Use the power of words in the direction of truth and love.

2. **Don't take anything personally.** Nothing others do is because of you. What others say and do is a projection of their own reality, their own dreams. When you are immune to the opinions and actions of others, you won't be the victim of needless suffering.

3. **Don't make assumptions.** Find the courage to ask questions and to express what you really want. Communicate with others as clearly as you can to avoid misunderstandings, sadness and drama. With just this one factor, you can completely transform your life.

4. **Always do your best.** Your best is going to change from moment to moment; it will be different when you are healthy as opposed to being sick. Under any circumstance, simply do your best, and you will avoid self-judgment, self-abuse and regret.

Conflicts in Relationships

There is bound to be disagreement over values, motivations, perceptions, ideas or desires in any healthy relationship. Conflict can provide opportunities to strengthen the bond between two people when it is handled in a respectful and positive way as it helps to clarify ideas, perceptions or our different perspectives in life. However, when a conflict is mismanaged, it may cause great harm to a relationship. In personal relationships, a lack of understanding and empathy about differing needs can result in break-ups whilst workplace conflicts may even result in broken deals or loss of jobs. When we can recognise the legitimacy of conflicting needs and become willing to attempt to examine them in an environment of compassionate understanding, it opens pathways to creative problem solving, team building and improved relationships.

Steps in Resolving Conflicts

- Starts with one party **taking responsibility to make amends.**
- **Engage in active listening with an open mind** to understand different perspectives.
- Take the opportunity to **clarify and exchange perspectives.**
- Be **non-confrontational;** increase your self-awareness and sensitivity to the feelings of the other party.
- **Be ready to repent and apologise.**
- **Be willing to collaborate and improve the situation.**

How Can We Resolve Conflict in a Relationship in a Constructive Way?

Conflict is inevitable with friends. There are occasions when we may disagree with one another's ideas. How do we resolve these "differences" in a positive manner and yet strengthen our relationships?

The SOLVED approach will be used to resolve the problem:

S   **State** the problem as you see it.
O   **Open** the discussion to other points of view.
L   **List** the possible solutions together. (Stress that illegal or harmful solutions are not even to be considered.)

V   **Veto** solutions that are unacceptable to someone involved. (If they are all unacceptable to someone, you may have to go back and think of more possible solutions.)

E   **Evaluate** the solutions that are left.

D   **Do** the one most acceptable to everyone.

Example

Jill and Joe usually go out on Saturdays. This Saturday, Jill wants to go to a movie while Joe wants to go to a party. Jill feels Joe just wants his own way all the time and isn't considerate. Joe thinks Jill is being stubborn. They are about to have an argument.

S   **State the problem as you see it.**

Jill: I am upset that you cancelled our movie day to go out with your friends.

O   **Open the discussion to other points of view.**

Joe: But I want to go over to Bill's house for the party as Bill is leaving Singapore.

Jill: I am upset that you didn't give me advance notice as I expected you to watch the movie with me on Saturday.

Joe: I am sorry for not giving you advanced notice. Maybe let's see how we can compromise on the time.

(Attempt to understand each other and what each party values.)

L   **List the possible solutions together.**

1. Jill could go to the movie with someone else while Joe goes to Bill's house.
2. They could go to the movie together and skip the party.
3. They could go to the party together and skip the movie.
4. They could go to the movie before or after the party.

(If the solutions are all unacceptable to both, they may have to go back and think of more possible solutions.)

V **Veto solutions that are unacceptable to someone involved.**
Solution 1 is unacceptable to both.
Solution 2 is unacceptable to Joe.
Solution 3 is unacceptable to Jill.

E **Evaluate the solutions that are left.**
Solution 4 is left and is acceptable to both. They find out when the
movie is playing and decide to go after the party.

D **Do the one most acceptable to everyone.**
They have fun at Bill's house and the whole group goes with them to
the movie afterward.

This approach may be acceptable between friends. However, if it is a family
conflict or between an employer and an employee, the solution may not
be acceptable to the child or the employee. However, there should be an
attempt to resolve the matter as best as possible so that there is a win-win
situation.

References

Ruiz, D. M. (2000). *Four Agreements Companion Book.* US: Amber Allen Publishing.
Gordon, T. (2009). *The Twelve Communication Roadblocks.* Retrieved from
http://www.unodc.org/ddt-training/treatment/VOLUME%20B/Volume%20
B%20-%20Module%202/3.Clinical%20Forms/3.T_Gordon_Roadblocks. pdf

Chapter 7

Making Responsible Decisions

Jessie Ee

Introduction

We make decisions every day e.g., What to eat? What to wear? Where to go? Who to meet? Which job to consider? Who to marry? the list goes on. How aware are we that we have made the right decision? Was it done on impulse or after a quarrel with someone or was it done in one of our bad moods? If so, how conscious are we that we have made a responsible and ethical decision? Some of our decisions worked out whilst some didn't work out. What actually goes wrong when some people make decisions? The two kinds of roadblocks to responsible decision making are as follows:

1. **Avoiding decisions** e.g., getting out of making decisions without even being aware that they are doing it.
   - **Drifting:** Just letting life takes its course without any goals in mind.
   - **Procrastination:** Waiting as long as possible without taking any action.
   - **Dreaming:** Spending time on wishful thinking.
   - **Being a back-seat driver:** Following what others do instead of thinking for yourself.
   - **Getting stuck:** Continuing what they're doing even when it's not working.
   - **Crashing:** Avoiding making decisions by acting up angrily or crumbling into a heap of tears.

2. **Using faculty thinking** e.g., using inappropriate thinking strategies that lead to poor decision making.

- **Being short-sighted:** Thinking only about what is happening right now.
- **Impulsiveness/hastiness:** Reaching conclusions and taking actions without sufficient thought, checking or attention to standards of judgement.
- **Narrowness:** Failing to consider other perspectives, the contrary evidence, alternative frames of reference and points of view, more imaginative possibilities, etc.
- **One way — my way:** Analysing situation in a way that is favourable only to oneself without thinking about the needs and desires of others.
- **Fuzzy thinking:** Lacking clarity in ideas or lacking sharpness to see distinctions.
- **Sprawling:** Lacking organisation in thinking; lacking focus — everything is all over the place.
- **Oppositional:** Doing the opposite, no matter what people suggest.
- **Not checking the "blind spot":** Something that you do not understand at all, often because you are not aware.

What is Responsible Decision Making?

To be responsible is to be accountable for our attitudes, words and actions and our ability to follow through what we have started, exercising self-control and striving for excellence and self-improvement. Responsible people tend to set good examples for others as they are able to plan ahead and be self-reliant, prudent, proactive, persistent and hard-working. They are aware of their roles in society and they act appropriately and maturely, assuming roles that are beyond what is expected. Responsible people also recognise the motives behind their actions, and they have the moral courage to reflect and own up to their errors to make the right choices or decisions.

Thus, responsible decision making is the active accurate involvement of assessing risks, evaluating and analysing the situation before making decisions, reflecting on pros, cons and the likely consequences of alternative courses of action, respecting others, and taking personal responsibility for one's own decisions. The value concepts are ultimately translated into action be it in improved communication skills, better decision making, and/or non-violent conflict resolution. This ability to make good decisions is a skill that comes from practice, experience and guidance from caring, responsible adults. Responsible decision-making skills are important in today's world where we are often faced with a variety of choices and opportunities.

Consider what these prominent people have to say on responsibility:

Action springs not from thought, but from a readiness for responsibility.

Dietrich Bonhoeffer (German Lutheran pastor and theologian)

Eventually we all have to accept full and total responsibility for our actions, everything we have done, and have not done.

Hubert Selby Jr. (Author of *Requiem for a Dream*)

The greatest day in your life and mine is when we take total responsibility for our attitudes. That's the day we truly grow up.

John C. Maxwell (Evangelical Christian author, speaker, and pastor)

What Are the Processes Involved in Responsible Decision Making?

Decision making is the act of choosing between two or more courses of action. It is not always easy to make the "correct" decision from among the available choices. Although decisions can be made using either intuition or reasoning, a combination of both approaches is often used. Whatever approach is used, it is usually helpful to structure decision making in order to

- break down more complicated decisions into simpler steps.
- see how decisions are arrived at.
- plan decision making to meet deadlines.

Many different techniques of decision making have been developed, ranging from simple rules of thumb, to extremely complex procedures. Two structured approaches will be introduced to assist the nature of the decisions. However, some basic processes must always be considered. They are as follows:

1. Identify the problem and analyse it. This requires our self-awareness of the problem, and we need to gather the facts of the problem. Questions to ask include

   — What was the source or root of the problem?
   — Who is involved?
   — What were their reasons?
   — How much time is needed to make the decision?
   — Who is responsible for the decision?

2. Establish the criteria or list the possible solutions as we think of different ways to solve the problem. This process could include brainstorming or some other idea-generating process, remembering to consider the possibility of not making a decision or doing nothing and being aware that both options are actually potential solutions in themselves.

3. Weigh the possible outcomes, bearing in mind the following questions:

   — What are the goals to be achieved?
   — What are the relevant criteria?
   — What are the pros and cons for each solution?
   — What are the predicted consequences (long/short range)?
   — What risks are involved (real/opportunity costs)?
   — What are the resources (available/substitute/constraints)?
   — How will it affect me and others?
   — Is it legal and morally ethical?

4. Decide on the values (self and others) that are important. This include considering the possible outcomes for now and the future as well as our own sets of beliefs concerning family, religion, friends, society, etc.

5. Evaluate by weighing and ranking alternatives in terms of selected criteria e.g.,
   — Risks
   — Unanticipated consequences
   — Strategies available to enact
   — Values

6. Choose the best alternative for implementation, bearing in mind the pros and cons of each course of action as timing may be critical.

Formats to Follow in Making Responsible Decisions

In our early years, rules set by our families help us in decision making. As children, we realised that we would have to face the consequences if we don't abide by the rules set by our parents e.g., "Homework before TV" or "No staying out late on a weekday". Other significant influences that we may encounter are our religious teachings, school rules, community laws and cultural traditions. Indirectly, these rules provide standards for acceptable and unacceptable behaviours and encourage one to be responsible.

In today's world, we are confronted with a variety of choices and opportunities throughout our lifetime. Responsible decision skills come from practice, experience and guidance from significant caring adults. Our beliefs and values are very much influenced by our experiences at home, school, workplace and the community at large. There is a need to recognise that there are possible consequences for every action taken. For example, if we are conscious in our purchases and note the difference between "needs" and "wants", we are less likely to spend lavishly as well as not accumulate "white elephants" at home. However, if we are not conscious of our spending, we may incur credit-card debts. Therefore, indirectly, the decisions we make may result in positive or negative consequences.

We may need to abide by some criteria in making responsible decisions regarding our choices of solutions e.g.,

- Is it harmful to me or to others?
- Is it wrong to do?
- Is it against the law, university rules or my religion?
- Would it disappoint my family or significant others?
- Would I be hurt or upset if someone did this to me?

In making responsible decisions, the above five questions may be another format used to guide our decisions. The above questions can be frequently referred to in the initial stages to assist us to respond more spontaneously. Each option **predicts** the consequences of the action. Having considered all the options and their consequences, it will allow us to **choose** the best course of action. We may **rethink** our decision after administering our decision and ask ourselves:

- How did things turn out?
- What must I do differently next time?

We need to be mindful that regardless of where the influence comes from when the decisions are made, we need to **own** the decision because we are rightfully responsible for the choices we make. It is not someone else's responsibility to make sure that we do the right thing. All our actions are a product of choice. It is our responsibility to make the right choice, the choice that is right for us as individuals, and the choice that has a positive effect. Below is a table for practice.

Making Responsible Decisions

1. Identify the decision to be made.

Should I study for my exam or go for a movie with my friend?
(You are welcome to replace the above question with your own.)

2. Think about the options. Throw out any options that are negative.

- Is it harmful to me or to others?
- Is it wrong to do?
- Is it against the law, university rules or my religion?
- Would it disappoint my family or significant others?
- Would I be hurt or upset if someone did this to me?

3. Predict the consequences of each positive option.

Options	Advantages	Disadvantages	Consequences	Evaluate Option
1				
2				
3				
4				

4. Choose and act on the best choice.

5. Rethink your decision.((How did things turn out? What should I do differently next time?)

Making Career Choices

According to Ee (2009), in making career choices, there may be more procedural steps to consider.

Stage 1: Steps for decision making

- Identify your interests and strengths (self-awareness).
- Consider the likely careers that suit your interest and strengths.
- Place ticks beside the interests and strengths related to the different jobs.
- Total up the ticks to discover the three likely careers.

Criteria→	Interests					Strengths					Total
Career ↓	music	children	math	reading	fashion	open to experience	sociable	flexible	linguist	caring	
Accountant			√								1
Teacher	√	√	√	√		√	√	√	√	√	9
Nurse		√				√	√		√	√	5
Fashion Designer					√	√		√			3
Lawyer					√	√		√	√		4

Conclusion: 1) Teacher 2) Nurse 3) Lawyer

Stage 2: Examine the pros, cons, consequences and reasons of your decisions.

- Set criteria e.g. housing, jobs, safety, etc.
- Consider the pros, cons, consequences and reasons for each criteria chosen.
- Rate the value on a scale of 1 to 5 (least to most).

Career: Teacher (Do likewise for the other two preferred careers)
Total: 23

Criteria	Pros	Cons	Consequences	Reasons	Values
Education	Needs degree	Needs financial support from parents	Pursue studies	Reputable degree is essential	5
Flexibility of Working Hours	School holidays	—	— More holidays than some careers — Can pursue areas of interest	Allows for destress	5
Salary	—	Not high salary	May have to consider a part-time job	Only bread winner in family	5
Career Advancement	Has prospects	Depends on principal in school	May consider part-time courses for advancement	Keeps me updated on education system	4
Work challenge	Every day is challenging and never boring	May be faced with difficult parents and supervisors	Stay focused on goals and improving communication skills	To explore my passion and keep me inspired	4

The above exercise will be repeated to assess the other two alternative careers.

The career with the highest ratings is the final choice.

Conclusion

In Chapter 3 and 4, you were introduced to two social emotional competencies related to the self (self-awareness and self-management). In self-awareness, you learnt about your strengths and limits and ways to strengthen your inner self whilst in self-management, you learnt about self-regulating not only yourselves but your emotions. In Chapter 5 and 6, you focused on others (social awareness and relationship management) where you learnt to develop empathy through reading others more accurately so that you could relate to them better. Chapter 7 allows you to use the four social emotional competencies so that you can make responsible decisions. In responsible decision making, you will realise the importance of recognising that for every action, there is a consequence. One has to reflect on and analyse the situation before setting criteria and listing the pros, cons and consequences of each solution to obtain the best possible solution that is ethical and morally right.

Making Responsible Career Decisions
Stage 1: Steps for decision making:

- Identify your interests and strengths (self-awareness).
- Consider the likely careers that suit your interest and strengths.
- Place ticks beside the interests and strengths related to the different jobs.
- Total up the ticks to discover the three likely careers.

Criteria → Career↓	Interests				Strengths				Total

Conclusion: 1)_____ 2)_____ 3)_____

Stage 2: Examine the pros, cons, consequences and reasons of your decisions.
- Set criteria e.g., housing, jobs, safety, etc.
- Consider the pros, cons, consequences and reasons for each criteria chosen.
- Rate the value on a scale of 1 to 5 (least to most).

Career Choice 1: _____ Total: _____

Criteria	Pros	Cons	Consequences	Reasons	Values

Career Choice 2: _____ Total: _____

Criteria	Pros	Cons	Consequences	Reasons	Values

Career Choice 3: _____ Total: _____

Criteria	Pros	Cons	Consequences	Reasons	Values

Best Career Choice is _____

Reference

Ee, J. (2009). Strategies for empowering metacognition through SEL. In Ee, J. (ed.), *Empowering Metacognition through SEL: Lessons for the Classroom*. Singapore: Cengage Learning Pte Ltd. Chapter 1, 3–24.

Part 3

Developing Work-Related Competencies at Home and in School

Chapter 8

Knowing Oneself
and Career Counselling

Ian Tan & Melvin Chia

Happiness is not having what you want, but wanting what you have.

~Rabbi H. Schachtel~

In her book *Happiness at Work*, Pryce-Jones (2010) calculates that workers will spend an average of 90,000 hours at work in their lifetimes. For the purpose of illustration, let us assume one works an average of eight hours a day for 260 days a year — this would translate to spending about 43 years at work! 43 years is about half of the average life expectancy in Singapore. The average person spends literally half of his or her life at work.

In other words, most adults spend more waking hours at work than anywhere else. It makes sense, therefore, to seek to find happiness and fulfilment in work since work occupies a large part of one's life.

There is an old Confucian saying that goes something like this:, "Choose a job you love, and you will never have to work a day in your life." On the individual level, the people who are most happy and fulfilled in their careers are those who have a good job fit. They are

- Aware of who they are, and happy in that knowledge
- Mindful of their motivated skills
- Clear about the way these skills will be helpful to the world

On the organisational level, with a good job-person fit, organisations reap tremendous benefits like a happy and engaged workforce who are committed to doing their best for their employers. If their hiring focus is on getting a good job-person fit, they can immediately develop their staff to achieve full potential without trying very hard and spending time to gain a better fit (Martin-Chua, 2014). In fact, in their book The *Power of Uniqueness*, Miller and Hendricks (2009) said, "By assessing people's strengths and deploying them accordingly, a company can more than triple their employee's effectiveness quotient."

By assessing people's strengths and deploying them accordingly, a company can more than triple their employee's effectiveness quotient.

~Arthur F. Miller~

Knowing Oneself

This begs the question of how you find a good job-person fit. "Who are you?" is a question you must ask yourself to be effective in your job search in finding the job you love. According to Drucker (2005), past history has shown that people generally did not manage their careers. More often, they relied on companies to chart their career paths. But in today's 21st century, we must all learn to manage our respective careers and shift our paradigm of "lifelong employment" to "self-responsibility for lifelong employability".

Drucker (2005) pointed out that few people actually know or take advantage of their fundamental strengths. Questions we need to ask ourselves include "What are my strengths?", "How do I perform?", "What are my values?" and "What should my contribution be?" A trained career counsellor will be able to help you answer these questions by identifying your unique qualities and support you in finding the right job-person fit. This usually involves the use of scientifically developed aptitude and personality tests.

Finding Your "Ideal" Work by Knowing Yourself

Is there such a thing as "ideal" work? Can one actually find it? We believe that the "ideal" work or good job matches are found at the intersection of a person's talents, skills, interests and values — all within the context of a unique personality (see Figure 8.1). Your ideal work would be found where all these come together (Taylor & Hardy, 2004).

"Who are you?" is a question you must ask yourself to be effective in your job search in finding the job you love.

1. Talent and skills (what am I good at?)
2. Interests (what do I like doing?)
3. Personality (who am I?)
4. Values (what's important to me?)

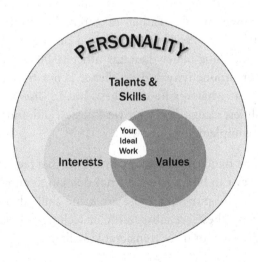

Figure 8.1: Finding Your Ideal Work

Source: Adapted from "Who Are You?" by Taylor & Hardy, 2004, *Monster Careers: How to Land the Job of Your Life* p. 74. Copyright 2004 by Monster Worldwide.

1. Talent and skills (what am I good at?)

One of the important things that employers looked for is how competent you are in handling the tasks that one is hired to do. We all have talents and skills but the real question is whether we have taken time to discover them.

Talents are natural, innate abilities. You know when you are engaged in your talent when you find the activity *energising, engaging, effortless, and enjoyable.* The thing you do is second nature to you. Perhaps you have a knack for persuading people or listening or in recognising patterns. Just imagine that the work you do engages your talents daily. Would you not be feeling motivated in doing what comes naturally to you?

> ಸೋಡಿ
>
> The Strengths Theory is based on the premise that every person can do one thing better than any other 10,000 people.
>
> ಸೋಡಿ

The Strengths Theory developed by Donald O. Clifton, an American psychologist known as "the Father of Strengths Psychology and the Grandfather of Positive Psychology", is based on the premise that every person can do one thing better than any other 10,000 people. The key in achieving greater productivity and excellence is not trying to be as good as someone else at whatever he does best, but in discovering your own exceptional abilities, recognising your weaknesses, and understanding how others' abilities complement your own.

Skills, on the other hand, are acquired capabilities that require time to hone and practise. They can be transferred from one job to another. Regardless of the career you are pursuing, there are some skills that are important to all employers — these are job-specific or technical skills. According to Goodwin (2015), some of these transferable skills are

1. Communication skills
2. Teamwork skills
3. Time management skills

4. Problem-solving skills
5. Organisation skills
6. Learning skills
7. Computer skills
8. Listening skills
9. Creativity skills
10. Leadership skills

2. Interests (what do I like doing?)

To make a good career choice, you need to know what you like to do. Potentially, your interests can lead you to many different professions. A person with an interest in music may decide to become a musician, but he or she may also become a disc jockey, choir director or music teacher. The key is to explore how your interest can translate into a career direction and how it relates to work. Imagine getting to do work that energises you and being paid for doing it!

3. Personality (who am I?)

Global learning institute Hyper Island conducted an internal survey of hundreds of industry professionals to find out the most desirable qualities in the leaders and workers of tomorrow. The findings which were released in 2014 revealed that "personality, not competence, is the determining factor of who's going to get the most attractive jobs among tomorrow's recruits". Having the right personality for the job is essential for businesses operating in a fast-changing digital landscape (Jerselius, 2014).

This does not mean that a skills set is not important. On the other hand, personality does play an important role in determining how one behaves in various settings, and has been linked to career development. Today's employers are selective about the candidate's personality traits when making decisions on offering employment. Assessment tools like DISC, Harrison Assessment, MBTI and Workplace Big Five are popular amongst employers who use them to assess candidates for selection. There is a saying that people are hired for what they can do but fired for who they are. Your personality is one of the key factors in finding a good job-person fit. It will be helpful for you to work with a career counsellor who is certified to administer the personality tests and help you discover more about you.

4. Values (what's important to me?)

Your values are internal motivators that affect your decision-making process and guide your life direction. It reveals what's important to you. The clearer you are of your values, the more powerful an influence they have on your decision-making process. They will influence the career choices you make as well as how you manage your career. If you want to be happy in your job, you need to find out how closely the job matches your values, as in personality, interests, talents and skills. For example, we know of people whose top values include "family" turning down well-paying jobs because these jobs require them to travel overseas and being away from their families, often for extended periods of time.

People get hired
for what they can
do and fired for
who they are.

Here is an exercise to get you started thinking about what is important to you. From the list below, write down your top five values in the space provided. Write a few words or phrases about what the values mean to you.

Accomplishment	Family	Predictability
Adventure	Friendship	Recognition
Affiliation	Fun	Respect
Artistic Expression	Harmony	Responsibility
Authority	Health	Risk-Taking
Autonomy	Helpfulness	Self-Discipline
Balance	Honesty	Service
Beauty	Humility	Spirituality
Challenge	Independence	Stability
Community	Influence	Structure
Competence	Integrity	Status
Competition	Justice	Teamwork
Contribution	Knowledge	Time Freedom
Control	Leadership	Trust
Cooperation	Learning	Variety
Creativity	Love	Wisdom
Curiosity	Loyalty	
Diversity	Meaning	
Duty	Money (High Pay)	
Faith	Pleasure	

My top five values are. . .

Value 1_____

Value 2_____

Value 3_____

Value 4_____

Value 5_____

Career Counselling and Its Benefits

This is where career counselling comes in useful. A career counsellor can help you to explore the answers to the four questions and compare possible jobs with your unique combination of qualities. You will discover new insights about yourself that will help you make important life and career decisions and lead to a better job-person fit.

To recap, the four questions are

1. Talent and skills (what am I good at?)
2. Interests (what do I like doing?)
3. Personality (who am I?)
4. Values (what's important to me?)

Besides helping you figure out who you are and what you want out of your education, your career and your life, the career counsellor provides you with useful industry information (e.g., industry trends, employment statistics, salary expectations, etc.) and advice to help you find a job. Here are five benefits of career counselling:

1. Assessing personal strengths and limitations

A trained professional in career counselling can provide you with various assessment tools such as DISC, Strong Interest Inventory and School Place Big Five to match your natural skills, strengths and abilities with possible career options. You will also find out your potential weaknesses so that you can avoid working towards a career that will only lead to frustration. Armed with this information, you can make wiser choices when making important life decisions including choosing which career path to take.

2. Goal setting for greater results

You will get help through the process of goal setting in your career choices by identifying the steps you need to take to reach your goals as you explore new career options or make changes in the career you already have.

3. Identifying choices in careers

You will be able to identify career options available today and focus on one area of a career path that works best for you. The career counsellor will help you to examine your occupational aspirations (loosely termed "dream jobs") as well as assess interests. Occupational aspirations have been known by psychologists as powerful predictors of future occupational activity (Reardon & Lenz, 1998) so that you work on realistic and motivating career goals that are right for you.

4. Educational support and guidance

You will also find support, resources and tools to help you achieve the training you need in the career to be successful in your new career path that may require specific training or education.

5. Job search support

The career counsellor is an invaluable source of support and resources when you are looking for a new job. Tactical support to help you find a job includes refining your resume and cover letter, and preparing you for the interview. The counsellor will be able to provide you with the tools, feedback and resources you need to be successful in your job search.

Knowing one's talents, skills, interests, personality and values is a very important factor in discovering a good job-person fit. It also helps an individual's career progress and advancement, leading to finding happiness and fulfilment at work. Going through the career counselling process will enable you to know and understand yourself and the world of work in order to make important career, educational and life decisions.

References

Drucker, P. F. (2005). Managing oneself. *Harvard Business Review*, 83(1), 100–109.
Goodwin, K. (2015). *Top 10 Transferable Skills*. Retrieved from http://www. careernotes.ca/employability/top-10-employability-skills/
Jerselius, A. (2014). *Personality Trumps Skills in Search of Talents*. Retrieved from https://www.hyperisland.com/community/news/hyper-island-execu- tive-study

Martin-Chua, E. (2014). *Creating the Fit.* Singapore: Singapore Institute of Management, 104.

Miller A. F. & Hendricks W. (2009). *The Power of Uniqueness.* Zondervan.

Pryce-Jones, J. (2010). *Happiness at Work: Maximizing Your Psychological Capital for Success.* Wiley-Blackwell.

Reardon, R. & Lenz, J. (1998). *The Self-Directed Search and Related Holland Career Materials: A Practitioner's Guide.* Odessa, FL: Psychological Assessment Resources. 13–28.

Tayor, J. & Hardy, D. (2004). *Monster Careers: How to Land the Job of Your Life.* Penguin Books.

Chapter 9

Getting the Most Out
of Industry Internships

Joel Lee

What are Internships?

Internships descended from professional apprenticeships that originated with the trade guilds of Europe in the 11th and 12th centuries. Master craftsmen and tradesmen, such as butchers, bricklayers, bakers, metallurgists, doctors and dentists, took in young learners and equipped them with specific skills of their trade, and these apprentices served one master for most of their teen years. Then they could graduate and start earning better wages.

This tradition of long-term human capital development continues in today's industry and education where the archetypal systems in Germany, Switzerland and Scandinavia are often quoted and modelled after. In today's immensely popular Dual System apprenticeship scheme in Germany, as much as two-thirds of their youths are involved upon completion of their secondary school education. The scheme allows them to learn any of the 374 professions available. Even those who gain admission to university prefer to undertake an apprenticeship before starting higher education at the university. Indeed, internships are an integral component of the German university system.

In Singapore's education system, industry internship, both local or overseas, has also been a key component of polytechnic education, where in general all final-year students spend three to six months on attachment with the industry to gain relevant on-the-job learning experience to complete their polytechnic education. The interns are conventionally paid an allowance of about $450–500 per month to cover transport and meals. For some diploma programmes, including nursing, pharmacy science and biomedical laboratory technology, students are provided grounding in the form of fundamental modules in their first year in the polytechnic before proceeding for an intensive two-year internship at a local teaching hospital. In short, depending on the course, polytechnics offer at least a three-month industry internship to the final-year student. This is in addition to the student completing a final-year project which could be done either in the polytechnic or in a company. If the latter, the student may in fact be working with the industry for a total period of six months.

Is There a Difference between Internships and Apprenticeships?

Both internships and apprenticeships require interns/apprentices to work with experienced people in a certain field and gain training under them. However, they are different in many ways. Apprenticeships are more intensive, usually lasting one to three years, and involve heavy training under an experienced, skilled and licensed professional to learn specific skills for a craft/vocation before the apprentices can start on their own. Apprentices can either be paid or unpaid, with many often unpaid. In contrast, internships are of shorter duration, e.g., three to six months and are often undertaken as fulfilment of a formal certificate programme in education. Unlike apprentices, interns undertake the professional attachment as a training programme for a white collar or professional career. People who opt for apprenticeships often already know that type of field they want to work in and are sure that they would not join any other field. Those who are on internship programmes will seize the opportunity to size up for themselves whether they would pursue careers in that field or enhance their on-the-job experience should they decide to do so.

What Can be Gained from an Internship?

In a polytechnic education, a student would be grounded in the fundamentals in year one of study. In year two, he or she would be studying more advanced modules and begin to apply and integrate the concepts and principles through critical thinking and problem solving, e.g., in written assignments and an industry project. Along with the development of the mind, the polytechnic student would at this stage be able to work individually or in teams, build up sufficient skills in communication and be resourceful enough to hunt for information from various sources. The internship in the final year three of a polytechnic education provides the opportunity to gain hands-on work experience that one just cannot get in the classroom. No amount of preparation for a career in a company is comparable to simply being immersed into the work culture, operations and environment of the company itself. During the internship, the student will pick up on-the-job work-ready skills such as interpersonal communication skills, relationship management, working across disciplines and across generations (e.g., reporting to senior management and working with peers as well as juniors), administrative duties, being responsible and confident in decision making, and "working smart". An internship can be seen as the pinnacle of one's polytechnic education and provides the chance for one to apply the knowledge and skills learned in the classroom in a real-world setting. It's a chance to prove the worth of one's training and validate that one can perform in the role assigned.

There is no doubt that the quality of the internship and what the student learns from that experience determine how much benefit he or she can gain from it. In the worst case scenario, interns can be physically and psychologically abused by company bosses, as seen in the case of a 17-second video showing how a boss of a local IT firm slapped a university intern. That video went viral on YouTube last year, incurring public outrage. The boss was charged with five counts of causing hurt to his intern employee, and one count of abusing the intern. Interestingly, even as the abused intern was leaving the IT company, he received four job offers, one of which had a monthly salary of $3,000, five times his previous intern pay.

These days, employers are usually as concerned with one's work experience as one's qualifications. For many of the more competitive jobs, internships, especially those involving relevant work experience, differentiate one job applicant from another. Indeed, internships provide graduates with an edge in the job market. It is not uncommon for companies to see interns as prospective employees, with some offering interns jobs upon successful completion of the internships. Interns can expect to transit into a job if they have proven themselves to be capable and hardworking and to get along well with the existing staff in the company. Just as companies give the interns a "trial run" during the internship to experience working in the companies, companies are doing "trial runs" of prospective employees when they host internships. So, if one is undecided about a career in a specific company, undertaking an internship can be a great and relatively short-term way to try it out without any commitment.

Internships are a great way to meet people in one's field. Even if you have gained some working experience, knowing people never hurts. An internship allows one to meet more people who might help one land a job later on and be the contacts in the industry you're trying to break into. Additionally, references from people in the industry will really add weight to one's job application.

Getting work experience from an internship is a great way to build one's confidence, thereby increasing chances of securing a job. What's more, even with an impressive resume, a solid internship experience allows one to impress job interviewers with actual deliverables supplemented with examples of how one innovatively overcame obstacles at work to solve problems as well as key positive learning points while working in the company.

Should One Opt for a Local or Overseas Internship?

In line with the growing internationalisation of Singapore's economy, with the development of a student's global awareness, and to prepare them for future overseas posting by employers, polytechnic students can choose to undertake an overseas internship instead of a local one. In going for an overseas internship, the interns have to look for an appropriate company overseas to be attached to for about three months. Interns need to consider cross-cultural challenges, be it food (e.g., will there be halal-certified food, vegetarian meals?), language (not only conversational but technical jargon at work if English is not used), need for a student work visa, cost of accommodation, security of location, ease of travel and learning opportunity. In view of these factors, interns tend to find work attachments for example with a Singapore company with overseas operations or with a multinational corporation (MNC) headquarters overseas. To some polytechnic students, the overseas internship may even be the first time he/she has travelled outside Singapore and for others, it could be their first time travelling without their parents and family. Based on feedback from MNCs and companies which have hosted local polytechnic interns overseas, a key impetus for companies to do so is for them to expose local interns to the culture and workings of the companies at their headquarters. Many of these companies with offices in Singapore are in fact on the lookout to hire local interns as full-time employees for their Singapore offices upon successful completion of their internships instead of posting their own staff from overseas to Singapore. Such companies are known to keep a database of interns who perform well when attached to their headquarters outside Singapore, and it is not uncommon for them to offer the former interns a job with their Singapore offices even two years post-graduation and after completing their National Service. While overseas internships have their advantages for interns, they often come at a cost. The polytechnics would have some form of financial assistance to help students of families with financial difficulties to cover the cost of a round-trip airfare, board and lodging, and insurance. An alternative strategy to allow more students benefit from an overseas internship is to send them to companies in countries closer home, e.g., within the more affordable ASEAN countries and China. Although working in some of these countries may not be as technologically advanced or fast paced as those in Europe and America, interns can still learn about working cross-culturally, developing businesses in emerging economies and lots more. There is no lack of learning value from internships overseas, no matter which country is chosen.

Do employers, university admission offices and scholarship panels pay attention to internship experiences in the resumes of job applicants, university applicants and scholarship applicants? Feedback from the industry, university admission offices and scholarship interview panels indicate that employers prefer outright those with overseas internship experiences and recognise their benefits. Many view those with overseas internship experience as showing more initiative and being more confident than their peers in their working experience, as well as demonstrating the potential in managing someone overseas and even illustrating a sense of adventure and risk taking despite uncertainties overseas.

What to Look Out for in Managing Quality Student Internship

Some employers believe that the current economy means companies have their choice of available interns. As a result, some companies have gotten lax in terms of learning what students really want in an internship. Hence, it is important for the polytechnics to do due diligence with companies, local and overseas, that are hosting student interns. To deliver quality student internships, polytechnic staff would often visit the companies, meet potential supervisors of the student interns and ask for a written job description of what the student interns would learn when attached to the company. Questions ought to be asked of whether the nature of the work during the internship matches what the interns would do should they subsequently graduate and decide to have a career in that company or field. In a tight labour market like present Singapore, polytechnics can ask companies to propose meaningful quality internship programmes for their students before deciding which companies they would send student interns to. Upon satisfaction that the objective of the internship is aligned with that of the learning objective for the students, the company is then listed as a possible venue for student internship. Other aspects for consideration include the work safety practice in the company, whether the student interns need to work shifts, any internship and overtime allowances, the company's commitment to training as seen by who they will assign to mentor/train the student interns, accessibility to the supervisor as well as liability issues when working in the company (e.g., what happens when the student accidentally contaminates a batch of sterile medical devices under manufacture). When a student interns with a company, the polytechnic should maintain regular contact with the intern via an industry liaison officer to ensure proper student welfare, ensure that there is learning value during the internship, and at the same time address any feedback and comments from the company on the student intern. It should never be the case that students are dumped onto the company hosting the interns and the students have to fend for themselves, especially if the internship is overseas. The polytechnics should have also worked with the company supervisor before the start of the internship on how to grade the students during the internship based on a set of rubrics or performance indicators. In many instances, companies may use student interns as extra pairs of hands and legs to supplement their workforce. There may be nothing wrong with this sort of deployment of student interns as long as they still get to do "meaningful" work, learning both about the business in general and acquiring the specific skills necessary to function effectively in the industry. However, should companies exploit student interns at work with little to no learning value, the polytechnics should have an alternative plan to redeploy the student interns to other companies which can do a better job in hosting meaningful student internships, and perhaps even blacklist such companies so that future batches of student interns do not suffer the same consequences.

Expectations of Internships in Singapore's Education Landscape

At the official opening ceremony of the Institute of Technical Education (ITE) Headquarters and ITE College Central on 8 November 2013, Prime Minister Lee Hsien Loong said,

> "To prepare our young, we have to make two important shifts. First, we have to focus more on applied learning — to integrate classroom learning with real-life applications on-the-job, and to encourage students to creatively apply concepts to practical problems …Secondly, we have to promote lifelong learning …and make this an attractive path for people."

Prime Minister Lee's point on applied learning and real-life applications on-the-job reinforces the important role of industry internship in providing on-the-job teaching and learning for our students. His speech also kick-started the formation of the Applied Study in Polytechnics and ITE Review (ASPIRE) Committee to review and recommend enhancements to the applied education model at the polytechnics and ITEs. Indeed, as the economy evolves and the economic environment becomes more dynamic and complex, demand for a wider range of skills, competencies and expertise will increase. What are the skills and competences that our students need to have in order to adapt and succeed in tomorrow's world? ASPIRE is focusing on strengthening polytechnic/ITE-industry linkages to (1) provide greater work-relevant training for students, (2) improve career and academic progression prospects for polytechnic and ITE graduates and (3) increase research, innovation and enterprise activities so as to ensure that current and effective teaching and learning support are provided to cater to the polytechnics' and ITE's academic missions.

At the Inaugural ASPIRE Student Townhall meeting held on 9 January 2014, Ms Indranee Rajah, the Chairperson of ASPIRE and Senior Minister of State, Ministry of Law and Ministry of Education, commented that unlike Germany, Finland and Korea have high unemployment rates amongst its university graduates. One of the key reasons for this is a mismatch between the job skills which are needed and the available supply of manpower. In contrast, Germany enjoys a relatively low unemployment rate. Amongst the many factors is their dual learning programme, which is an apprenticeship programme. She highlighted that in Germany, students have on-the-job training provided by companies as well as classroom instruction as taught in the vocational schools. Apprentices typically spend one to two days a week in schools while the remaining three to four days are spent in the companies. Consequently, this work-study programme offers a very close relationship between applied/practical learning and theoretical learning. Even as the ASPIRE Committee is in the process of refining and consolidating its recommendations at the time of writing this chapter, what is apparent is that one of its recommendations would encompass launching work-study programmes with industry to deepen skills training in polytechnics and ITE students so as to better prepare them to be "work ready". Under such a programme, industry internships would be lengthened beyond the present three months to six months or more. Polytechnics and ITEs would collaborate with industry to allow the latter to teach student interns on-site in the company what used to be taught in the final year in the lecture theatres and laboratories in polytechnics and ITEs. Student interns would also be assessed and graded by the company. A number of industry sectors have been selected to pilot the work-study programme to be launched from 2015 onwards. Looking forward in conclusion, industry internship will continue to feature in an even more intense way in the teaching and learning in the polytechnics and ITEs.

Chapter 10

Employability Skills
in Career Preparation

Agnes Chang

Education policies and reforms in Singapore are underpinned by employability and national growth. Hence, career guidance is indirectly planned even in the primary classes.

Many parents are still of the mindset that getting admission into an elite school and getting a degree will ensure a good position with a comfortable salary. Times have changed with Singapore being a globalised city and a hub for international investors. Employers are now looking beyond paper qualifications and technical skills in their recruitment of employees. They are looking for applicants with problem-solving skills and soft skills. Singapore University of Management, National University of Singapore and Nanyang Technological University have launched courses to prepare their graduates for employment.

A number of research studies have been conducted in the United States on employability skills, and a comparison of these studies by Cotton (1993) has been organised into three categories — basic skills, higher-order thinking skills, and affective skills and traits.

Basic Skills

- **Oral communication (speaking, listening)**
  The expression "speech maketh a man" means that being able to communicate is extremely important at interviews and in meaningful interactions. Oral language assessment is an important aspect of language assessment at all levels in school to improve students' communication skills. Class presentations are a common feature in academic subjects. Heavy weightage is also allocated for pre-university project work presentations.
  In relation to good communications is mastery of languages. In Singapore schools, the medium of instruction is English, and the mother tongue (Chinese, Malay, Tamil) is mandatory. The mother tongue policy has placed Singaporeans in an advantageous position in securing positions in ASEAN and Asian countries like China, Taiwan and Hong Kong. Other countries are adopting the bilingual policy as well in order to improve employability opportunities for their growth. In *The Sunday Times* (9 February 2014), Melissa Sim reported that more children in the United States are learning Chinese as parents recognise the benefits of learning the language as the Chinese economy grows. Similarly, British Prime Minister David Cameron encouraged British children to learn Chinese.

- **Reading,** like oral communication, is related to language mastery and is especially crucial for understanding and following instructions. Reading goes beyond books and written media. In this digital age, forms and documents are often completed online.

- **Writing** is a very powerful aspect in daily communication on paper or online, for personal interaction or formal communication. Good reading habits help to improve writing skills.

- **Mathematics** is an educational requirement at every level in every programme in Singapore schools. The syllabus covers all topics including algebra, geometry and other abstract topics which are offered as electives in some countries. Singapore has attained high scores in international competitions like Trends in International Mathematics and Science Study (TIMSS) and Programme for International Student Assessment (PISA).

Many jobs available are science and technology-based, and mastery in numeracy will be an advantage in securing jobs.

- **Information Technology**
  Singapore is one of the countries with the "best-wired" classrooms. Information technology (IT) allows quick communication "just a click away". We are moving onto the Fourth IT Masterplan and we are encouraging the use of ICT in teaching and learning. Plans are occurring to have "future" classrooms. Hence, IT literacy is an important asset in a person's curriculum vitae.

- **Specialised Skills and Knowledge**
  While it is not necessary to be a degree holder to land a job, it is important to possess special skills and knowledge to make one employable. While David Gan and Sam Leong do not possess an "O" level certificate, they are specialists in the skills of hairdressing and up-market cooking, respectively. One must acquire a skill or knowledge that makes one a valued member of the community.

Higher-Order Thinking Skills

Higher-order thinking skills include the following:

- Adaptive problem solving
- Learning skills and strategies
- Critical thinking
- Creative, innovative thinking
- Responsible decision making
- Helicopter view

Many unpredictable changes are taking place across the world, impacting on business and employment opportunities. Prime Minister Lee Hsien Loong and the Minister for Education, Mr Heng Swee Keat, have repeatedly stressed the necessity for students to move away from rote learning and to develop critical thinking and creative solving skills. Likewise, employers need to engage workers who can assist them to solve existing problems and spot potential problems, and who can learn new skills and knowledge to expand businesses.

In 1997, the then Prime Minister, Mr Goh Chok Tong, launched the Thinking School, Learning Nation initiative which underpins all the subsequent educational policies and reforms. Assessment has been revamped to evaluate thinking skills and problem solving. Recently, Singapore has topped the PISA assessment in problem-solving skills of 15 year olds.

Besides adaptive problem solving, responsible decision making is one of the key goals of teaching thinking skills. Flexibility is necessary in problem solving, depending on the culture, available solutions and persons involved. Responsible decision making is imperative for the successive execution of plans.

Helicopter view is the ability to size up potential opportunities and develop future plans. Every individual needs to envisage his or her future career and work towards the goals set. Similarly, employers need to have workers who have good foresight or vision to help expand the business for the company.

Affective Skills and Traits

Interpersonal skills and team spirit are highly valued in workplaces as group work and collaboration between different departments and companies are the characteristics of modern workplaces. Excellent academic results alone do not ensure leadership qualities in a recruit. A leader must be able to lead, motivate subordinates and cooperate with other leaders in the company. The following affective skills have been identified as essential for successful employability:

- **Dependability/responsibility**
  It is important to have a positive attitude towards work. The positive attitude of colleagues can affect the working climate of a company.

- **Conscientiousness, punctuality, efficiency**
  Punctuality is one trait on the watch-list of employers who usually mark it as an item for work evaluation.

- **Interpersonal skills, cooperation, team player**
  Successful teamwork brings about productivity while in-group conflicts will lower work morale and productivity. Good interpersonal skills will promote staff retention and loyalty.

- **Self-confidence, positive self-image**
  Self-confidence is an important asset at job interviews and sends a positive and convincing image to interviewers.

- **Adaptability, flexibility**
  In problem solving, skills and knowledge alone may not help in finding a solution unless skills and knowledge are adapted to the culture and needs of the clients. Flexible use of skills and knowledge is the key to adaptive problem solving.

- **Enthusiasm, motivation**
  In the United States and Canada, students have listed enthusiasm and motivation as the most desirable characteristics of teachers. Enthusiasm is always seen as an energising force in any workplace.

- **Self-discipline, self-management**
  Management of one's emotions is always considered a plus point for any job. Positive attitudes, interpersonal skills and enthusiasm are connected to self-discipline and self-management.

- **Appropriate dress grooming**
  Many job seekers have not considered appropriate dressing as an important aspect of employability. One of the grooming lessons for Singapore University of Management (SMU) undergraduates is how to dress for a job interview. Employers have commented positively on SMU applicants in this aspect. A potential bank employee should not turn up for the job interview in a mini-skirt, a see-through blouse and sandals. Similarly, we would not like to see "would-be" teachers in short shorts and tight T-shirts at their interview. It was reported that a girl in Hong Kong turned up in shorts and Japanese slippers for her job interview and was told to leave immediately. Dressing indicates one's respect for self, the interviewers and the profession.

- **Honesty, integrity**
  Character is the most important consideration for all employers in their selection of new recruits. That is why applications must be accompanied by character references. Knowledge and skills without integrity are the makings of a ticking time-bomb for any company. Trainee teachers who were caught cheating in one way or another (e.g., changing the date of medical certificate) were given immediate dismissals by the Ministry of Education as it undermines the reputation of the teaching profession.

- **Ability to work without supervision**
  Independence is linked to dependability and responsible decision making.

In *The Straits Times* (19 May 2014) Amelia Teng wrote on life skills being taught to primary pupils to prepare them for adulthood. These skills include the following:

1. Leadership
2. Motivation
3. Teamwork
4. Public speaking
5. Entrepreneurship
6. Business skills
7. Financial literacy
8. Basic dining etiquette
9. Presentation skills
10. Problem solving
11. Communication

The above life skills can be provided by external vendors through games and group activities. This signifies the importance of learning social and interpersonal skills at a young age.

In conclusion, it is never too early to start guiding students to acquire the necessary skills and knowledge in preparing them for employment and being an acceptable and contributing member of society. Applied learning is not only meant for secondary and tertiary students. It should start at primary levels as early inculcation of values and skills will set a solid foundation for life.

References

Cotton, K. (1993). *Developing Employability Skills.* Northwest Regional Educational Laboratory. Retrieved on 15 July 2005 from http://www.nwrel.org/scpd/sirs/8/ c015.html

Sim, M. (2014). More kids in US learning Chinese. *The Straits Times,* 9 February 2014, p. 20.

Teng, A. (2014). Children pick up grown-up skills in school. *The Straits Times,* 19 May 2014, B1, p. 13.

Chapter 11

Networking Through Collaborative Learning

Agnes Chang

Introduction

Group work is a common and must-have activity in schools at all levels. To some students, group work, sharing, negotiating and presentations are necessary evils in school learning. They do not understand they are learning and practising collaboration skills through cooperative teamwork.

Collaborative learning is the first step towards learning to network later on in life. Networking to many is a word symbolic of "business" or "politics". This is very unfortunate as networking is crucial for all vocations at all levels, from cleaners and clerks to managers, teachers, doctors and professors to company CEOs. Many professionals feel that they can do well in their careers without connecting with professionals from other fields as they are too busy to socialise. But there is no excuse now, as networking can be done within seconds with a click of the computer mouse.

Networking is beyond "marketing oneself". According to some business giants, networking is not a luxury but a necessity. Though companies normally advertise in their recruitment for staff, the management often shortlists the applicants according to the recommendations of trusted referees whom they know and respect. Even publishing a research paper in a journal depends on the academic status of the writer or on how well he or she is known to the publisher.

Though networking is so critical for business growth and career advancement, the management of many organisations and institutions in Singapore do not encourage networking through attendance at forums, conferences and invitations to competitors' events. The fear of these organisations is the leakage of "secrets" to competitors through "loose cannons" among their staff. But productivity is more than being tied to the computer and the phone.

The Importance of Networking As an Essential Skill in the 21st Century Workplace

Networking to most youngsters is being popular, with a collection of "likes" on Facebook and plenty of social media mail. A quick review of the exclusive summer management courses at top Ivy League universities shows that the curriculum consists of sessions of networking with participants from countries around the globe. These networking sessions cost more than US$10,000.

Our ministers, including the Prime Minister, communicate and connect with the citizens via Facebook. Professionals around the globe connect through LinkedIn. There are five important reasons to network:

1. Making connections for work and creating opportunities outside work
2. Getting complex things done in a simple manner, with assistance from others
3. Increasing knowledge by exchanging information and ideas
4. Increasing concentration by collaborating with others
5. Rallying support from others

Ways to Network

It is important to note the following points when networking:

1. Show interest in others. Have an open and curious mind about the person you are talking to.
2. Give value to others. Share ideas and information that benefit others.

3. Connect because you care, not for personal favours. Insincerity shows up and kills connection.
4. Benefit your network first, not your personal agenda.
5. Forge long-lasting relationships through personal notes, greeting cards and meaningful emails.

Networking can be achieved through

1. Collaboration through projects
2. Discussion over a cup of coffee or tea (especially to colleagues and neighbours)
3. Use of the phone more often than emails (especially to colleagues, faculty members and friends)
4. Attendance at seminars, conferences and talks conducted by organisations related to your interests, studies and work
5. Taking part in community work and charitable events to connect with people from different walks of life
6. Distribution of name cards at events and functions and follow-up with emails/phone calls
7. Use of newspapers, journals and books as a good avenue to connect with people you are interested in
8. Being members of respectable social media or professional organisations

Killing Networks

The following are surefire ways to kill networking attempts:

1. Oversell yourself by talking non-stop about your achievement.
2. Network for a personal agenda.
3. Dress inappropriately for networking occasions. (Networking occasions are not meant for distractions — appropriate dressing reflects one's good taste, knowledge of protocol and etiquette.)
4. Wait for others to approach or introduce you. (You should always make the first move to introduce yourself.)
5. Make a beeline for the most important or best dressed persons in the room. (It is good to have a goal, but do not turn people off with overly obvious intentions.)

6. Hog a conversation and ignore the others around you. (You should always try to include everyone in the same conversation group.)

Learning to Network in School

Until recent years, interpersonal skills and networking were not considered top of the list of skills for students at the primary, secondary and post-secondary levels. These skills were meant for tertiary institutions. However, the need for group work, cooperation and collaborative learning was recognised in the late 20th century. Our students were noticed for not being able to communicate fluently and eloquently. Hence, opportunities have been created for more oral interactions and the use of oral presentations during school hours. A higher weightage is also assigned to oral presentations, as in the "A" level project presentations.

It is sad that some students, parents and even teachers are ignorant of the goals and long-time benefits of group problem-based learning (PBL) or project work. Through the objective of achieving a good grade for a pre-university group project, the following skills are hopefully learnt and retained:

1. Cooperation
2. Collaborative learning
3. Sharing
4. Listening skills
5. Critical thinking
6. Creative problem solving
7. Negotiation skills
8. Empathy
9. Interpersonal skills
10. Respect for others' ideas and opinions
11. Perspective taking
12. Maximising the strengths of each member in solving the problem

In modern workplaces, all the above skills are highly valued for teamwork to ensure productivity. The display of selfish self-serving actions from any one member of a group will cause unwanted flaws in the final product. Unless students, parents and teachers understand the critical need for the cultivation of team spirit in group work, it is difficult to move ahead with the development of higher-level networking skills.

In group work, the art of listening to, and learning from others, starts with intelligent humility and the belief that there is always something to learn from others. The essence of networking is to share, learn, improve and connect. If a person believes that he is the best, and there is nothing to learn from interacting with others, he is closing his own window to advancement and enlightenment.

Group work is introduced in kindergartens, and desks in the lower primary classes are arranged to ensure group interaction. Young children are egocentric, and working in groups at a young age initiates children into learning to share and cooperate. A number of Singapore schools go beyond the classroom to inculcate social and interpersonal skills like public speaking, teamwork and presentation skills in their pupils by employing external vendors (Teng, 2014).

Unfortunately, cooperation is often sabotaged by aggressive competition, especially in schools where top results are the ultimate goal of students, encouraged by ambitious parents. Little do these parents realise that they are preventing their children from developing skills critical for employability.

The Ministry of Education is making changes not to highlight top PSLE scores to "cool" the preoccupation with scores and grades, and has sent popular principals to schools which are not known as elite schools. Project work and problem-based learning are widely encouraged in the state high schools to promote critical thinking and collaborative learning. Singapore tertiary institutions including polytechnics are advocating problem-based learning to engage students in academic interactions and collaborative learning.

Schools are creating opportunities for students from across Singapore to network through interschool games, music festivals, band competitions, debates and science quizzes. However, these opportunities are frequently overshadowed by the push for the students to win for the schools. The more important objective of promoting interschool goodwill and friendship is often downplayed.

Conclusion

Learning to develop social skills and to interact with the intention of developing good relationships need to start from a young age. Networking does not belong to the business sector exclusively. Teachers need to network with other teachers in the same school and across other schools in order to learn new pedagogical strategies. That is why the Ministry of Education organises Teachers' Conferences every other year. Professors network via journals and professional websites to gain information in the latest research of their specialisations. Musicians attend the concerts of other music makers to learn and advance their skills and knowledge.

Networking is a professional skill that can bring you forward in your knowledge, skills and career. We have heard of head-hunting for talents by professional companies. Unless you are known among your peers for your expertise, you will not be attractive to potential employers and research partners. Hence, you need to make your expertise known to people who may be interested in your skills and expertise by networking.

References

Seah, Y. C. (2014). Improve your networking skills. *The Straits Times*, 30 January 2014, c10.

Teng, A. (2014). Children pick up grown-up skills in school. *The Straits Times*, 19 May 2014, B1, p. 13.

Chapter 12

Building Confidence and Resilience

Esther Tan

Introduction

Resilience is broadly understood as positive adaptation in circumstances where difficulties — personal, familial or environmental — are so extreme that we would expect a person's cognitive or functional abilities to be impaired (Masten & Coatsworth, 1998). Simply put, it is bouncing back from crisis and becoming stronger and better, ready to face new challenges. A more scientific term for resilience is adversity quotient (AQ). AQ is not new. The term gained recognition and popularity with the publication of a book entitled *Adversity Quotient* written by Paul Stolz 18 years ago. According to Stoltz (1997), AQ is a measure of how a person responds to adversity positively and, as a result, improves overall personal and professional effectiveness. He believes that an individual's success in life and at work is largely determined by his or her AQ which predicts

1. How well a person withstands adversity and his or her ability to surmount it
2. Who will overcome adversity and who will be crushed
3. Who will exceed expectations of their performance and potential and who will fall short
4. Who will prevail and who will give up

Stoltz (1997) asserts that there is a relationship between AQ and academic success. When students make conscious efforts to tackle academic problems and take positive actions to solve them, they can increase their self-esteem and motivation to complete tasks, and ability to succeed in academic pursuits. Hence, the higher the AQ, the more likely an individual is able to overcome adversity and succeed in life.

There have been concerns among educators and parents in Singapore that our youth are too sheltered and over-protected, and, as a result, lacking in resilience. Many are "softies" who do not persevere when given challenging tasks, and who are prone to give up in the face of failure. The good news is, local research findings have revealed that the majority of secondary school students in Singapore have positive strategies in coping with stress. In a local study by D'Rozario and Goh (1998), it was shown that secondary students in a sample of government schools coped with stress by seeking relaxing diversions; using problem-focused strategies that focus on the positive aspects of their work; using physical recreation; and seeking social support. Also, social and emotional learning (SEL) programmes introduced into Singapore schools since 2007 has sought to promote self-awareness and self-confidence among students, facilitate the development of interpersonal and social skills, and enhance decision-making and problem-solving skills. Two research studies by Ee and Zhou (2012) and Ee (2013) showed that both primary and secondary school students' self-awareness, social awareness, self-management and relationship management skills predict responsible decision making. Furthermore, the students' thinking and self-esteem mediates between their social emotional competencies and achievement. Ee and Ong (2014) further found that even the parents in the experimental group were able to note the improvement of their children who went through the SEL programmes.

Youth studying in our post-secondary and tertiary institutions often face many challenges, not only in their academic pursuits, but also in their interpersonal and social interactions with their peers, teachers and family members. What can they do to enhance self-confidence and build resilience? This chapter attempts to offer some answers to these questions.

Findings of the International Resilience Project

One way to find answers to these questions is to study the findings of credible research projects. In 1993 the Dutch Bernard van Lee Foundation funded an international research project to examine what parents can do to promote resilience in children. The study involved 589 children and their care givers from 14 countries, including Asian countries such as Thailand, Vietnam, Japan and Taiwan. The study found that to overcome adversities, children in the sample drew from three sources of resilience features that the researchers labelled I HAVE, I AM, I CAN (Grotberg, 1995).

I HAVE

- People around me I trust and who love me, no matter what
- People who set limits for me so I know when to stop before there is danger or trouble
- People who show me how to do things right by the way they do things
- People who want me to learn to do things on my own
- People who help me when I am sick, in danger or need to learn

I AM

- A person people can like and love
- Glad to do nice things for others and show my concern
- Respectful of myself and others
- Willing to be responsible for what I do
- Sure things will be all right

I CAN

- Talk to others about things that frighten me or bother me
- Find ways to solve problems that I face
- Control myself when I feel like doing something not right or dangerous
- Figure out when it is a good time to talk to someone or to take action
- Find someone to help me when I need it

The researchers also found that a resilient child does not need all of these features to be resilient, but one feature is not enough. A child may be loved (I HAVE), but if he or she has no inner strength (I AM) or social, interpersonal skills (I CAN), there can be no resilience. A child may have a great deal of self-esteem (I AM), but if he or she does not know how to communicate with others or solve problems (I CAN), and has no one to help him or her (I HAVE), the child is not resilient. A child may be very verbal and speak well (I CAN), but if he or she has no empathy (I AM) or does not learn from role models (I HAVE), there is no resilience. Resilience results from a combination of these features.

The Foundation Stone of Resilience: Self-Confidence and a Positive Self-Concept

Although the participants of the International Resilience Project were children below 12 years old, we can draw a few lessons from the findings of this research study in our discussion on promoting resilience in youths.

It is obvious from the literature as well as from research findings that one basic ingredient for building resilience is a healthy and wholesome self-concept. Self-concept shapes the way a person interprets experiences and events that he perceives. It acts as an inner filter where every perception is given a meaning by the individual, determined largely by the view the individual has of himself. If a person has a negative view of himself, then every experience is likely to be interpreted in a negative light. For example, a friendly invitation may be mistaken as a challenge and a compliment misconstrued as an insult in disguise. On the other hand, if a person has positive self-esteem, each experience is perceived in a positive light and stamped with a smile rather than a frown.

Generally a positive self-concept can be equated with positive self-evaluation, self-respect, self-esteem and self-acceptance. Self-esteem reflects a person's overall emotional evaluation of his or her own worth. It is a judgement of oneself as well as an attitude towards the self — the notion that "I am a worthy person; I am able and capable; I can learn; I am willing to try; and I can succeed". It goes without saying that individuals with a positive self-concept are more prepared to face new challenges and take risks. They are also more likely to persevere in the face of difficulties and setbacks and do not give up easily. In short, they are resilient people.

How does one build a positive concept and develop confidence? The first thing to do is to find a sense of purpose in life. Basically, this involves finding answers to these questions — Who am I? What am I good at? Why am I here? What can I do to contribute to life and society? Answering these questions usually leads to the establishment of life goals, both short-term and long-term goals. For a student still undergoing training, the short-term goals may be related to his or her studies and the long-term goals pertain to his or her career plans and life goals. Establishing life goals helps to give us a sense of direction in life. When we have life goals, we have a sense of direction and that can prepare us to take up challenges and face difficulties.

The second task is to discover our potentials and strengths and work on these to achieve our goals. When our goals are realistic, chances of success are good. When we complete a task successfully, we feel a sense of satisfaction and achievement and that helps to boost our confidence. When we are confident, we are ready for the next challenge. Building positive belief in our abilities is a great way to build resilience for the future.

The Building Blocks of Resilience: Positive Mental Health and Physical Wellness

A healthy self-concept is often linked to the development of a positive outlook in life, and optimism is a powerful weapon to fight setbacks and stress. Positive thinking does not mean ignoring the problem. It means understanding that setbacks in life are transient and believing that one has the abilities and means to combat the challenges one is facing.

While developing a positive self-concept and establishing life goals are important for our personal growth and mental health, we must also establish a positive attitude towards change. Flexibility is an essential part of resilience. By learning how to be more adaptable, we will be better equipped to respond when faced with setbacks and difficulties. While some people may be crushed by abrupt changes, resilient individuals are able to adapt and thrive.

There is a positive relationship between mental health and physical wellness. Good physical health — and a regular routine of healthy habits — are fundamental to both mental and emotional resilience. Thus, while we nurture our mental health and build a positive attitude to life, we also need to take care of our physical health, not just through eating wholesome food, but also through having regular exercise and getting enough sleep. Daily habits count. When we are sleeping, eating and working well, we will be able to keep fit physically and mentally and are less fragile when under stress or facing challenges. Thus nurturing our physical and mental health is an important part of building resilience.

Protective Factors in Building Resilience

Stresses in life are inevitable, and every individual will face challenges in life at one time or another. The good news is, there are protective factors we can rely on in building resilience. These protective factors can be described as "qualities or situations that help alter or reverse expected negative outcomes". When an individual faces setbacks in life, the presence of these protective factors can help him or her cope with the situation positively and effectively. These protective factors can be internal (from within the individual) or external (involving the family, school and community).

In a sense, positive self-esteem and an optimistic outlook to life discussed above can be seen as examples of internal protective factors. Another protective factor an individual can cultivate is to keep on learning and improving oneself through upgrading courses and lifelong learning. Keep working on your existing skills, be they study skills or work skills but especially your problem-solving skills. Research has shown that people who are able to come up with solutions to a problem are better able to cope with problems than those who cannot come up with solutions. Whenever you encounter a new challenge, make a list of the potential ways you could solve the problem. Experiment with different strategies and focus on developing a viable option.

External protective factors come from a caring family, a safe learning environment and a supportive community; in other words, from developing and establishing a strong supportive social and emotional network.

Researchers have identified three themes involving external protective factors — caring relationships, positive and high expectations from significant others, and opportunities for meaningful participation.

Having caring, supportive people around you acts as a protective factor in times of crises. It is important to build a social network and have people you can trust and confide in, who will lend a listening ear in times of trouble and a shoulder for you to cry on. As the saying goes, "Happiness that is shared is doubled but sorrow that is shared is halved." While simply talking about a situation with a friend or loved one will not make the troubles go away, it allows one to share feelings, gain support, receive positive feedback and come up with possible solutions to the problems.

Other family protective factors may include (1) a caring relationship with a family member; (2) warm, structured and positive discipline practices at home; (3) parental monitoring and supervision; (4) a stable home environment which provides opportunities for youths to contribute to family goals; (5) family quality time with each other and (6) support from the extended family. All these family protective factors highlight the power of strong relationships. In fact, studies of resilience have found that the most significant factor in overcoming adversity is a long-term relationship with a caring adult. A positive relationship with a significant other is the number one predictor of positive outcomes among people who face extreme circumstances.

Schools can help students develop resilience by providing a positive and safe learning environment, along with setting high, yet achievable, academic and social expectations. Community protective factors include neighbourhoods that offer a context where youth can be exposed to positive influences. Some examples of community support factors are after-school programmes, community team projects that provide opportunities to explore potentials and develop leadership qualities, and wholesome recreational activities that promote physical and mental health.

An Action-Based Approach to Promoting Resilience

Stoltz (1997) suggested that one way to promote AQ or resilience is to learn the LEAD sequence. This approach is based on the notion that we can alter our chances of success by changing our habits of thought. The approach involves four simple steps to deal with adversity.

1. L = Listen to one's response to the adversity. Essentially this means developing the ability to recognise and assess the crisis that is happening.
2. E = Explore all origins of the crisis and your ownership of the result. Origin means identifying and accepting blame for causing the adverse situation (like failing an important exam because you did not work hard enough to prepare for it). Ownership of the result means holding yourself accountable for doing something to deal with or resolve the crisis situation, even if you did not cause it.
3. A = Analyse the evidence. This involves a simple questioning process in which you examine, dispute and eventually derail the destructive or negative aspects of your response.
4. D = Do something. This is not compulsive action, but action based on critical thinking and rational planning.

Characteristics of Resilient Youths

Resilient youths are self-confident and maintain a positive outlook on life. They approach people and situations with hope, faith and trust. This can come about only if they have positive self-esteem, self-acceptance and acceptance of others. When significant adults in their life show unconditional love and emotional support, accepting them as they are with their strengths as well as limitations, they will feel safe and secure, that they are worthy, accepted and loved. They are able to say, "I am a worthy individual and a lovable person. I am surrounded by people I can trust, who support me emotionally and love me unconditionally."

Self-acceptance leads to acceptance of others. Resilient youths with positive self-esteem are also very positive and caring in their attitude towards others. They possess social and interpersonal skills to help them communicate and get along with others. They are able to express their thoughts and feelings and can show empathy and compassion for others. Such social and emotional competence helps them in developing a supportive social and emotional network.

Resilient youths have acquired internal locus of control. They are self-reliant, motivated to learn and proactive , being able to plan ahead. They are able to control their impulses and manage their emotions. They can make decisions, take responsibility for their actions and learn from their mistakes. They are able to say, "I am responsible for what I do and I am proud of what I have done."

Resilient youths are also risk takers, ever ready to take on new challenges. They are persistent doers rather than instant quitters. They have moral pride and a sense of humour. They persevere in their efforts and do not give up easily in the face of failure. When it comes to coping skills, resilient youths are effective problem solvers. They are resourceful, knowing when, where and how to seek help when they need it.

Conclusion

Changes are inevitable in life; so is stress. It is therefore paramount that all of us build resilience to help us weather the storms in life. Psychologists believe that resilience is a basic human capacity which is nascent in all of us. In others words, we all have the potential to be resilient; only, this innate capacity needs to be cultivated and nurtured to be fully developed.

A multi-pronged approach is required to help build resilience in our youths. While a youth's own genetic make-up and temperament may affect his or her way in perceiving and dealing with challenges in life, he or she can develop resilience through fostering a positive self-concept, adopting an optimistic outlook to life, learning interpersonal and problem-solving skills and building a social network as a safety net. As significant others in their life, parents and teachers play a pivotal role in lending social and emotional support and serving as positive role models in their own quest for resilience.

References

Crawford, L.E.D. & Chua, T.T. (2000). Promoting adversity quotient among Singaporean school children. *REACT*, June, 10–4.

D'Rozario, V. & Goh, M. (1998). How adolescents cope with their concerns: A review and study of Singaporean students. *REACT,* 1, 13–20.

Ee, J. (2013). *Equipping Secondary Students with Metacognitive and Social Emotional Competency Skills to Meet the Challenges of the 21st Century.* Research report. Singapore: National Institute of Education.

Ee, J. & Ong, C. W. (2014). Which social emotional competencies are enhanced at an SEL camp? *Journal of Adventure Education and Outdoor Learning,* 13(1), 1–18.

Ee, J. & Zhou, M. (2012). *Empowering Metacognition through Social Emotional Learning.* Research report. Singapore: National Institute of Education.

Grotberg, E. H. (1995). A guide to promoting resilience in children: Strengthening the human spirit. *Early Childhood Development: Practice and Reflections* series. Bernard Van Leer Foundation.

Masten, A. S. & Coatsworth, J. D. (1998). The development of competence in favorable and unfavorable environments. *American Psychologist,* 53, 205–229.

Stoltz, P. G. (1997). *Adversity Quotient.* New York: John Wiley & Sons.

Chapter 13

Fostering Critical Communication Skills for the Future

Jeffrey Mok

The stage was set. A press conference was about to get underway. A group of excited scientists sat next to each other facing a crowd of news reporters and media personnel. Among them was a young scientist, who was the leader in the research team that discovered the world's first superconductor. As the press conference got underway, attention turned towards another person, the senior researcher and spokesperson of the team. Because he was more eloquent and able to present the results in a clearer and more persuasive way, the senior researcher got the most questions and requests for clarifications about the discovery. But he was not the person who had worked hard with the team of researchers to make the breakthrough in this most coveted engineering innovation. Even though he repeatedly credited the younger scientist as the team leader who discovered it, the media continued to give him the attention. History went down to record this senior researcher as the person credited for the discovery. This episode demonstrates the critical importance of communication in the workplace.

Communication in the workplace is always a challenge. You have your work cut out for you, and you give your best in terms of ideas, hard work and performance. Yet, these efforts never seem to be enough unless the ideas are communicated to the people who evaluate you. Your hard work and performance, if they are somehow not spoken to or reported to the people that matter, will go unnoticed. In the workplace, communication skills are seen by companies and organisations as the most powerful element to possess as a skills set. When you search the classified advertisements for jobs, you will invariably come across "Good/Excellent communication skills" as a requirement for all entry-level positions. In fact, in order to progress and climb the corporate ladder, the ability to communicate in order to network and negotiate is an essential ingredient.

This chapter is about communication and what it means to you. As a young person heading into the future with a life full of work, play and leisure, being able to communicate well is a skill that every youth needs. Communication skills have been identified as one of the critical skills (AACTE, 2010) that no young person growing up should be left untrained in order to survive in the 21st century. Recognising and doing something to your communication style will put you in a commanding position for the rest of your life. What you are about to read (or discover) is going to change your life. This chapter will reveal to you fundamental facts about communication and life. The earlier you hone your communication skills, the better you will be.

You are Only as Good as You Communicate

The first life-changing fact is that your ideas, efforts and performance are only as good as you can communicate them. Have you heard of the saying, "A person can have the greatest idea in the world — completely different and novel — but if that person can't convince other people enough, it doesn't matter"? You may not know the person who said this but understanding this message is like discovering a gigantic pot filled with gold. This quotation is saying that unless you are able to communicate what is in your head, no matter how fantastic your idea is, it is useless. In other words, when you are pit against another person with the same quality of ideas, the difference lies in whoever has the ability to explain it better. There are countless examples where those who can speak better get the prize. You can probably recall instances in your life where your friend (or rival) who spoke better than you got the better deal. The earlier true story of the press conference of the discovery of the world's first superconductor is a case in point to show how crucial good communication is in presenting ideas to people. The scientist who actually discovered the superconductor did not speak as well as the others. The one who spoke well, even though he repeatedly said it was his colleague who discovered the superconductor, instead got his name mentioned and plastered all over the papers as the one who invented it (Pool, 1988). Therein lies the irony: the person who deserves to get the recognition after all the long hours of hard work, was not recognised just because he could not communicate well enough. So the first life-changing fact is that we have to work on our communication skills if we want to be recognised.

Everything You Say or Do is Your Public Image

We can dress nicely and appear sophisticated but once we open our mouths, our real person comes out. There is a saying that captures this brilliantly in a funny way: "Since light travels faster than sound, people appear bright until you hear them speak." The way we speak creates the public image people have of us. This is because the way we speak (and write), i.e., how we communicate, tells others who we really are. Our values, preferences, ideas, amount of knowledge and level of maturity are all revealed when we open our mouths. So what we say and how we say them, speaks volumes of the person that we are. They reveal the real you. I lived in Japan for six years, and as an Asian with Chinese ethnicity, I look very much the same as any of the Japanese walking on the streets. In fact, as long as you dress and behave like them, nodding frequently and observing polite behaviour, I can be mistaken for a Japanese. The reality, that I am a non-Japanese, is revealed once I open my mouth to speak at length, even when I am using the Japanese language. It is not just the odd pronunciation here and there but it is the manner of expressions and perspectives that are clearly not spoken in the way the Japanese expect it. And that is when the Japanese would begin to treat me differently — as a non-Japanese.

In the workplace, we can (and should) dress nicely and appear to be important but when we speak our minds, our speech and manner begin to create the image others have about us. In the cut-throat environment of the working world, it is often said that "he who shouts the loudest, gets heard". This is often true if the management only notices the loud voices, but there is a deeper underlying truth in that saying. It is saying that whoever has the ability to get noticed, in sound bites, gets recognised. Of course, we are not only talking about speaking but also writing. So, your communication need not be loud, but if you managed to get the attention, spoken or written, of your bosses or people that matter, your ideas and even you will be noticed. So everything you say or do is *your* public image. Our professional image in our workplace may be first created visually by our appearance, but it is eventually determined by what we say (and do).

So, how do we work on our communication skills such that our ideas, efforts and performance can be recognised? What can we do to our communication skills such that we can project ourselves well enough for others to take notice and regard us in a good light? First, the good news is that communication is a skill, and as a skill it can be learnt.

Communication is a Skill

Communication is seen as an intentional activity in conveying information and meaning to another using various means. And any intentional activity can be learnt and mastered. While some of us will say that we are not born with the language ability to be effective communicators, we need not despair. Language ability certainly helps in communication but it does not *guarantee* effective communication. A person who is fluent in the language may not be necessarily effective in getting the message across. This person may not be clear in delivering the message. Have you watched on television how someone appears to speak fluently but at the end of his speech, you have no clue what the person is saying exactly? This is often the case when people are asked to give a comment or response on the spot without any preparation. In this case even those who can speak fluently can appear to have said nothing concrete at all. A person can also be longwinded and talk more than necessary, or use colourful expressions but the ideas and thinking do not flow logically from one point to another. So, while the language ability helps, it is ultimately how you craft the message that matters more. Do not despair if you think you do not have a good command of the language. We start from wherever we are and learn how to craft our messages and present them in the most effective way. The following sections will show you how.

Take Any Advantage to Learn to Speak and Write Well

When we talk about communication, what comes naturally to mind is the ability to speak and write well. This is why thousands of families are sending their kids to language schools and additional tuition after class. However, not everyone of us has the privilege of having access to additional language classes or communication courses. Certainly, if we have a communication coach or language teacher to improve the way we speak and write, we can definitely begin to communicate better. Because communication is a skill and all skills require practice to improve, it is clear that we need to practise and learn as often as we can.

In Robert Kiyosaki's New York Times bestseller *Rich Dad, Poor Dad* (Kiyosaki & Lechter, 2000), one tip to be financially independent was to take advantage of whatever circumstances you are in. One of his examples was to live off a "rich dad" for as long as you can without incurring unnecessary expenditure. This was his way of capitalising and maximising whatever privileges or opportunities you have to gain financially. This same advice applies here: if you are given opportunities in school or at home to learn how to speak and write well, take full advantage of them. If you have classes in language and communication or are surrounded with people who speak or write well, learn as much as you can from them. If you are currently enrolled in a communications class, pay extra attention and ask questions on how you can improve your skills. If there are extra or elective courses on communications, elect to take them. Or if you have a relative or friend whom you think communicates very well, learn from him or her. So, take a moment to examine the unique circumstances you are in and see how you can leverage off them to improve on your communication skills.

If You Have to Choose, Choose Speaking

Not all of us can speak and write well at the same time. Some of us can speak better than write; others are better at writing than speaking. Depending on our preferences and circumstances, how we were brought up in our families and the exposure we have, we develop these two productive skills of communication differently. The more exposure and practice you have with either skill, the better you are. However, research has shown that we speak more than we write in life and clearly, if we are going to do a lot of speaking than writing, we should focus on our speaking skills. Bear in mind that this is regardless of whether we are female or male. In fact, we speak two to three times as much as we write in the workplace (Bovee & Thill, 2013). When we meet somebody new, our first impressions are formed when we see the person and hear what comes out of his or her mouth. We do not get the chance to "show off" our written skill when we meet people face to face. Even if we are impressed by the emails or writings of a person, how often are we "disappointed" when we meet the person and find that he or she speaks poorly? How often are we also let down when the good-looking person or famous personality that we admire so much starts to open his or her mouth? Somehow, being able to speak well has a higher standing than writing. It is one of our human biases — we tend to fall for a good talker far more than for a good writer.

So, if we have to concentrate on improving one of the communication skills, we should start with speaking. Being able to speak clearly and concisely is one of the first principles of good communication. Besides speaking clearly and concisely, we also need to be persuasive and convincing when we talk. This means that we need to position the key messages at the right places and emphasise them with stresses and pauses. One excellent speaker to learn from is the late Steve Jobs. Watch his presentations on his Apple products and observe how he varies his tone, positions his key points, stresses and pauses. While we fully understand that not all of us can speak like Steve Jobs, it will not hurt us if we begin to pay attention to how we speak and talk to others (Gallo, 2009). If we can speak better than we did last year or even five years ago, it'll be a boost, not just to our self-esteem but also to others' impression of us.

Speaking Alone is Not Enough

That is right, you read correctly. Speaking on its own is insufficient to carry the ideas and messages across to our listener. Have you noticed the difference between listening to the news and listening to a story being told on radio or television? Which medium comes across more memorably or easier for you to understand? We all know the answer to that, and it all has to do with this fascinating fact about communication: body language increases the effectiveness of your spoken words by 55% and the quality of your voice (tone and inflection, etc.) can bump it up to another 38% (Mehrabian & Wiener, 1967). What this means is that the communication of your message does not rely on your words alone! Your body language and the way you say your words speak louder than your words can do on their own. That is why we have to really concentrate when we are listening to the radio as compared to when we are watching television. Watching the person talk enhances the communication many times and we can pick up the information without much difficulty.

Body language when speaking refers to facial expressions, hand gestures and movements, and the tone and inflection of the words highlighting the stresses as well as the pauses. All these other "tools" are ways to support and enhance the words that we speak in order to effectively convey the message to our listener. It is also one of the reasons why it is a lot harder to lie to a person face to face compared to lying over the phone. If body language can enhance speech by 55% (Bovee & Thill, 2013) and paralanguage (tone and inflection, etc.) can enhance it by another 38%, we should be using these for maximum effect when speaking. A good example is to use our fingers to show the number when we mispronounce the number "three" (Singaporeans love to pronounce it as "tree"). Or pause before making an important point and stress the key words with a raised tone. In other words, develop good body language skills to support our average speaking skills so that we can still effectively convey the message we want to send.

If You Want to Write Well, Read Lots

I can see some of you raising your hands, saying that you really cannot or do not want to speak well and you prefer and can better express yourself in writing as you are more of the introvert type. Well, there are many successful personalities who are introverts (Cain, 2013) and do not like to be the centre of attention because they cannot speak well. To improve on writing skills, one tip is to read more. In fact, there is research showing a strong relationship between reading and writing (Stotsky, 1983). When we read more, we tend to be able to write better because we are more exposed to good sentences — provided you are reading good books (comics and magazines do not count). The research showed that students who read more turned in better-quality essays and had higher written assignment scores, and this was shown at both primary and secondary school levels. So, one of the easier ways to improve your writing is to read and especially, read in the same area that you intend to write.

Speaking and Writing Is Secondary to Something Else!

In reality, whether we speak or write, it is not how loud we can speak or how flowery is the written language. It is something more than those things and unless we speak and write with this in mind, we can never communicate well to our audiences. It may surprise you to realise that among the four language skills — reading, writing, speaking and listening — we *listen* a lot more (one-and-a-half to two times more than speaking (Bovee & Thill, 2013). So if you are serious about communicating well, learn to listen well and you will be able to speak (and write) well too. It was Zeno of Citium (if you are into Greek philosophers) who once remarked, "We have two ears and one mouth, so we should listen more than we say." And what listening does is that we listen first before we speak, thus placing the focus on understanding and reading the audience first before we communicate. This is actually the crux of communication: audience centeredness. Before we speak and write, we need to consider the audience's preferences, likes and dislikes, and how best to communicate to this audience.

Whether we are speaking to our parents, friend, classmate, colleague or boss, the very same message is communicated in different ways, ways that can best convey the message not just effectively but persuasively. By listening to, and observing, the person you want to send the message to, we can utter words that can speak straight to the heart of that person. For instance, if the person prefers the soft approach, we should use gentle and sensitive words when we speak or write to that person. Or if the person likes facts and figures, we should fill our messages with numbers and factual statements to not only get that person's attention but to convince him or her. So, before we open our mouths or pen that first word, considering the audience first will go a long way towards achieving good communication.

All Workplace Communication is Persuasive

This is another important fact that we need to recognise. Because all, if not most, communication in the workplace revolves around work, we are constantly required to make our ideas, perspectives and even information appealing to others. In short, we have to *sell* our ideas, perspectives and information. We have to bring the other person to our point of view in order to get our work done. In an example of a simple request for more information on a project from a colleague, we need to "convince" him or her to provide the information. If we have power over the person, we will have an easy time to get the person to do the task not only well but also quickly, such as when the boss instructs a subordinate to do something. But if there is no power play involved and we are on an equal footing, we need to speak or write the request in such a way that the person will be "persuaded" to do it for us. Otherwise, the request will be added to person's long list of "to do" items and you can be sure that it will be a while before the request is attended to. (Unless the person likes you!) Of course, there are more examples — such as when presenting your project work, making proposals, or sharing your ideas in a meeting — when your communication needs to be persuasive. Being persuasive in your speech or email writing, has become an essential feature in the workplace.

Having highlighted some of the important facts about communication, I will now turn to suggesting some techniques to help us be more effective in our communication. I will share how we can be more persuasive, clear and concise in our communication.

Be persuasive

To be persuasive requires us to be effectively audience-centred in our thinking. This means that we need to think about our audience and figure out how best to reach out and connect with the person we are communicating with. The first technique is the "You" attitude in our messages. The "You" attitude requires us to communicate from the person's perspective or expectation when the person receives our message. In other words, if the person expects us to be polite, positive, personal and professional in our communication, we should communicate accordingly. If the person expects us to be respectful of his or her values, orientation and preferences, we should demonstrate these qualities in our communication. When we speak or write from the audience's perspective and expectations, we will quickly get his or her attention and also persuade the person to our point of view. So, if we communicate politely, positively, personally and professionally, and are respectful of the person's values, orientation and preferences, we can be very persuasive.

Be clear

Clarity in your communication is a fundamental trait. You have read earlier that a good command of the language may not necessarily mean you can be clear in your communication. You can communicate clearly at any level of language ability as long as you know how to do it. The first technique is to **keep your communication simple**. Albert Einstein once said this: "If you can't explain it simply, you don't understand it well enough." The great scientist who dabbled with complex scientific questions and complicated mathematical issues has nailed communication on its head — be simple. And when your communication is simple, it will be clear. Being simple means using familiar and easy-to-understand words in your speech or sentences that are accessible by most people. In fact, many institutions such as the legal community, medical bodies and business associations have been seeing a communication revolution in their institutions. They are toning down their jargon and levelling their sophisticated language to make their communication plainer and simpler for the man in the street. So avoid difficult words and try not to impress people with complex words and expressions.

The second technique is to **use "picture words"**. This means using words that are not abstract but words that paint a picture in the minds of the listener or reader. Instead of saying "the cost of living has increased by a lot", you can say "increased by 20%". The more numbers or visual images that your words can conjure up for your audience, the easier it is for the audience to understand. If I want to say that the person is nice, I can say that the person thinks of others first. If we have to use abstract terms, follow up that word with a picture word. So if I want to say that the job was easy, I can follow that up with the phrase "easy as ABC". By doing this, we are in fact communicating with the receiver in mind. We are helping the receiver of our messages to easily understand our words. We are audience-centred in our communication.

The third technique is called **positioning**. To make our communication clear, we position the very thing we want to say at the very beginning. In other words, the main message comes in front of everything else we want to say or add to the message. This is also known as **being direct** in our communication. We do not waste any time nor let our audience infer or second-guess what we want to say in the first place. Place your key message either in the first sentence or at least in the second such that the listener or reader gets the message at the beginning. We can also repeat the key message throughout the time we are speaking or in our writing. To be really clear in our message, we can conclude with the same key message at the end of our speech or writing. In a sense, we are repeating the main message over and over again. We do this to all important messages, don't we? If we want someone to listen to us and not miss the point we are making, we always say it at the beginning and repeat it again later. If there is a fire in your house and there is someone in the room oblivious of the danger, you would shout to the person the important message to get out. You can give the reason that there is a fire in the house but you will repeat the main message again — to get out of the house. This is your way of ensuring that the person gets the message regardless of anything else. Similarly, in our communication, if our key message is so important that the listener or reader needs to get it, we must make sure the person gets it at the first hearing or reading. We position the key message in front.

Be concise

Remember in the earlier section when I mentioned that a person can have good language ability and be fluent and yet be ineffective in communication? Besides being unclear, the person can say a lot of words and not get to the point. Being longwinded or taking a long time to get to the point is another way to be not effective in your communication. When you are concise in your communication, you are not only a good communicator, you are saving people's time. Being concise is also being direct in communication which in turn makes your message clearer. How many times have you suffered over someone's longwinded speech or laborious writing and wished the person would have stopped a long time ago? You either have gotten the message already or worse, you are still waiting for the main message to surface. Such communicators, even though they may have a good command of the language, have failed to consider the audience in their communication. In workplace communication, besides clarity, conciseness is the next most valued quality in any form of communication. This is because time is precious and we have a lot of other important things to do rather than wait for the person to finish the message.

There are two ways I want to share with you to be concise in your communication in this chapter. The first one is to ensure that there is no redundancy in your communication. If you can say the message with fewer words, do that. In speech, Singaporeans love to use redundant words such as "basically", "actually" and "all right" even though these words do not add additional meaning or information to the messages they are conveying. Apart from these unnecessary insertions in our spoken language, we also add needless words in the front or at the back such as "my personal opinion", "after two hours later", "return back" and "we finished already". To be concise, we need to be precise and brief in what we want to say. In the written form, for example, we can remove one of the words in "free gift", "prompt and speedy", "absolutely necessary" and "added bonus". While there are many examples of such redundant words in speech, there are also many such words in writing that we can shorten to keep to the key information we want to communicate.

The other way to be concise is to use strong and active verbs instead of passive ones. Strong and active verbs make the message clear by putting the subject of the message as the main actor. Using active verbs allows the subject and action of your subject to be clearly visualised. They describe the action directly and are more concrete. Remember "picture words"? In this way, there is little doubt or ambiguity to what you want to say in the message. Also, the active form uses fewer words than the passive form. For example, instead of saying "New procedures have been implemented to ensure …", say "I implemented new procedures to ensure …". Using active verbs and cutting down redundant words will ensure that your messages are concise and in turn, make them clear as well.

I have shown you how to be persuasive, clear and concise in your communication in order to be effective. However, there are circumstances when we want to be unclear, indirect and longwinded. These circumstances are when we want to weasel out of a difficult situation or want to deliberately appear ambiguous — then we can be unclear and ramble along to mask the real message. We can be ineffective in our communication because we have a different goal to achieve: not to get the message across quickly.

Communication and Trust Are Two Main Ingredients for a Successful Relationship

We have talked about the importance of communication skills in the workplace and some surprising facts about communication to shape our perspectives in life. We have also been shown some useful pointers to improve our communication skills, especially on how to be persuasive, clear and concise. While it is good to know its importance and ways to improve it, it is also useful to know the goal of communication. One of the goals in communication is to establish and sustain good and successful relationships. In fact, being able to communicate is the starting point of any relationship and clearly the foundation to maintain any relationships. When my father wanted to remarry after my mother had passed away, I asked him whether they loved each other. To my surprise, my father responded with a simple statement: we can communicate with each other. At that point, I did not fully understand how communication could replace love, but now I have come to realise that one of the key ingredients of a loving relationship is the ability to communicate. A good foundation in communication is not just the basis for a good marriage but also for all forms of communication. Our friends remain as good friends because communication is sustained. How often have we heard stories of how relationships are strained or broken because of communication break down? The success of social media tools such as Facebook and Instagram hinges on the fundamental fact that humans love to connect and by connecting, we continue our relentless communication with each other. Therefore, if we really desire our relationships to be in good shape and to grow deeper, we really need to work on our communication skills whether it is at our workplace or even at home.

References

American Association of Colleges of Teacher Education and the Partnership for the 21st Century Skills (AACTE) (P21) (2010). *21st Century Knowledge and Skills in Educator Preparation.* Retrieved from http://www.p21.org/storage/documents/aacte_p21_whitepaper2010.pdf

Bovee, C. & Thill, J. (2013). *Business Communication Today,* 12th ed. Harlow: Prentice Hall.

Cain, S. (2013). *Quiet: The Power of Introverts in a World That Can't Stop Talking.* New York: Crown Publishers.

Gallo, C. (2009). *The Presentation Secrets of Steve Jobs: How to Be Insanely Great in Front of Any Audience.* New York: McGraw-Hill.

Kiyosaki, R. & Lechter, S. (2000). *Rich Dad Poor Dad: What the Rich Teach Their Kids About Money That the Poor and Middle Class Do Not!* New York: Warner Business Books.

Mehrabian, A., & Wiener, M. (1967). Decoding of inconsistent communications. *Journal of Personality and Social Psychology,* 6(1): 109–114.

Pool, R. (1988). Superconductor credits bypass Alabama. *Science,* 241: 655–657.

Stotsky, S. (1983). Research on reading/writing relationships: A synthesis and suggested directions. *Language Arts,* 60(5): 627–642.

Chapter 14

Sharpening Your Resume Writing and Interview Skills

Adelaide Chang

Why You Need to Learn to Write a Resume and to Have a Successful Interview

Job hunting is a highly adventurous process. You are racing against the odds to land that desired, much needed job. Writing an impressive resume and the ability to be interviewed confidently are vital in this race. Both resume writing and performing well at interviews are skills that can be cultivated and sharpened. In this chapter, you will be exposed to two types of resumes and learn what to do before, during, and after interviews. At the same time, you will be taught how to write an acceptable cover letter that introduces your resume to a prospective employer.

What is a Resume?

A resume is not an autobiography nor is it a chronicle of all your experiences. It should summarise experiences relevant to your career goals and what you have learnt from these experiences, and highlight your achievements.

The resume is a marketing tool. It should sell you to prospective employers the same way an advertisement entices you to purchase a product. It is the first impression that employers have of you and from it they will decide on whether they will call you for interviews.

Basic Types of Resumes

There are two basic types of resumes:

1. Chronological resume (better known as curriculum vitae or CV). The CV is an in-depth document that covers two or more pages and contains a high level of information about your achievements. It also covers your education as well as other accomplishments such as publications, awards and honours.
2. Functional resume. The functional resume is a highly customisable document which highlights your skills and accomplishments in specific areas such as administration, quality control, marketing, etc. Normally, it is only about one page in size and is useful for those candidates who are re-entering the job market after a work gap or those who are changing careers. It is to their interest to change their resume from one job application to another to focus on the needs of the specific post.

Keys to an Impressive Resume

The main objective of a resume is to entice the recruiting manager to read it and to give you an opportunity to be interviewed. The four keys to an impressive resume are

- Simple, elegant design
- Strong focus
- Specific and detailed information
- Authenticity

To make resumes stand out, the following features are suggested:

- Use white paper.
- Have good page margins.
- Separate different sections to avoid cramming things together.
- Avoid fancy graphics.
- Do not use glamour shot photographs.
- Use standard fonts (e.g., Arial 12 points).
- Avoid fancy bullets and long lists of bullet points.

- Avoid excessively lengthy resumes.
- Check that your grammar and spelling are correct.
- Couch your facts in a neutral or slightly positive way in order not to sound negative.

What are the Essentials to be Included?

Important information to be included in your resume are

1. Name, complete mailing address, telephone number and email address. The more accessible you are, the more likely that you can be reached.

2. Career objective to indicate the type of jobs that you are looking for. It serves as a sense of direction for you, the job-seeker. It should be specific enough for you to know what you are looking for, but not so rigid that you would not be considered for a wider range of positions available.

3. Education.
   - If GCE "N", "O" or "A" level is your last graduation, include that.
   - If you had graduated from an ITE or polytechnic, include that.
   - If you have Bachelor's, Master's and PhD degrees, include all three but go back no further.
   - Include the name and location of the institute of higher learning (city and country), major fields of study, subject of major research, date of graduation, academic honours and bursaries/scholarships obtained (if any).

4. Employer-sponsored courses and on-the-job training received in current or past employment.

5. Work history and experiences including skills and accomplishments. You need to indicate your achievements and how well you performed in your previous jobs.

6. Professional associations and memberships.

7. Specific skills that you have acquired such as language proficiency.

8. Hobbies and interests can be mentioned if they can help you to secure the job.

9. References can be submitted if they are requested and they can help you to secure the job.

What to Emphasise if You are Composing Your First Resume

Very often, people composing their first resume worry that their part-time jobs, holiday jobs and internship attachments are not impressive enough to potential employers. This is not necessarily the case, especially if you can frame your experiences in a way that calls attention to skills that are transferable from one work environment to another.

When listing your previous jobs, do not simply list the job title and description. Mention responsibilities that required you to work under pressure and tight deadlines, interact with customers, show initiative or supervise other employees. For example, in many service jobs, more experienced employees are required to mentor newer employees when they start work. This can be phrased on the resume as "responsible for training new employees on customer service policies, operation of computers and company policies, or whatever tasks they may have to handle".

If your work experience is limited, you can emphasise your academic-related accomplishments, This should go beyond grades and include co-curricular activities such as club committees, athletics, and charitable activities, and anything else that demonstrates your leadership skills or that is directly relevant to your career goals.

You should also list achievements and experiences that you have racked up outside of school or work. This might include travel, volunteering, involvement with civic organisations or memberships in community or religious groups. All these activities tell employers something about you and your ability to commit and interact in your community.

Example of chronological resume (curriculum vitae)

Name: Wendy Cheng Wan Yee
Address: 15 Thomas Drive
            Singapore 249320
Tel: 67339753
Email: wendych@singnet.com.sg

Objective

A position as a Senior Engineering Assistant that is challenging and will lead to greater opportunity and more responsibility

Education

2012   Completed Diploma in Marine Engineering at
        The Singapore Polytechnic
1999   GCE "O" Level with 5 "O" level passes from the
        River Valley Secondary School

Work Experiences

2012–Present   Engineering Assistant at the Robin Shipyard

— Responsible for the shipyard's statistical reporting to the Singapore Government.
— Established inventory control.
— Implemented fiscal control to cut down on waste.

Example of functional resume

Name: Ann Kwok
Address: 15 Margaret Drive
            Block 2 #06-23
            Singapore 123456
Tel: 67347022
Email: annk@gmail.com

Career Objective

A secretarial position that is challenging and will lead to greater responsibility and opportunity

Skills

Typewriting: 50 words per minute
Well versed in the Microsoft package of Word, Excel, PowerPoint and Outlook

Education

GCE "O" Level from Geylang Methodist Girls' School, 1998
GCE "N" Level from Geylang Methodist Girls' School, 1996

Experiences

Assistant Secretary

2000–Present RCA where I support the Manager of Financial Recovery Department. Composed correspondence and was responsible for record management. Coordinated and compiled diverse information (semi-annual reports), trained junior staff and explained concepts. Coordinated financial documents such as cheques and letters of credit from travel agencies. Communicated and updated agency terminations, accounts and bankruptcy claims.

Administrative Assistant

1998–2000 Colgate Corporation where I assisted the Executive Secretary in the organisation of meetings and conferences, created and maintained file systems, prioritised assignments and implemented ideas and strategies. Familiar with word processing, faxing, sending of telexes and handling of telephone correspondence.

The Cover Letter

In a job application, the cover letter introduces you to your prospective employer. A good introduction entices the reader to review your resume. A well-crafted letter, together with a carefully prepared resume, represents your best chance of securing an interview.

A good cover letter takes no more time to type than a weak cover letter. Furthermore, time that you spent in composing a good cover letter pays back many times as you can use the facts and phrases in other application letters.

Often, employers select job applicants who not only have the required skill or potential but who can communicate well. View cover letter writing as an opportunity for you to demonstrate your writing skill to a potential employer.

Tips in Composing Cover Letters

1. Type each letter individually. Do not mass produce the letters as you are writing to different potential employers whose requirements differ from each other.
2. Never photocopy your letter as it shows that you do not care and are not interested in doing a proper job.
3. If possible, address the employing officer by name and by title. Research names via the library or company website, or call the company directly.
4. Catch the employer's attention by opening your letter with a strong statement. An employer receives hundreds of application letters per month and you would want your letter to be the one that is read.
5. Keep your letter short and sharp. It should not exceed one-and-a-half pages with five to six paragraphs.
6. Arouse the employer's interest by stating brief facts about your experiences and accomplishments which will add value to his company.
7. Keep the tone of your letter positive and upbeat.
8. Be direct in requesting for a reply and an interview.
9. Sign and date your cover letter.
10. Use justification for even right-hand margins.
11. Check and recheck for spelling and typing errors.

Example of a cover letter

Block 38 Tampines Street 11
#07-44
Singapore 499290

23 January 2015

Mr Patrick Sng
Human Resource Manager
Tian Wah Publications Pte Ltd
87 Upper Bukit Timah Road
Singapore 290322

Dear Mr Sng

APPLICATION FOR POST OF SUBSCRIPTION OFFICER

Communication skills are the key to success for the post of Subscription Officer that you had advertised for in the *Straits Times* on 20 January 2015.

My expertise in the following areas qualifies me for the position:

- Excellent oral/written English and Mandarin
- Ability to speak major Chinese dialects and Malay
- One year's telemarketing experience with Readers' Digest
- One year's experience promoting sports wear
- One year's administrative experience in a retail operation
- Diploma in Business Studies from the Ngee Ann Polytechnic

The Subscription Officer position is in line with my career goals as spelt out in my attached resume. I would like to meet up with you and discuss on how I could contribute to your organisation at your earliest convenience.

Best regards,
Elizabeth Chua

What Constitutes a Good Interview?

An interview is a framework or structure to provide responses. The main objectives of an interview are to

1. Evaluate a candidate in an accurate and fair manner in order to identify the right candidate who will add value to the organisation
2. Treat the candidate in a courteous and professional manner such that he or she will have a favourable impression of the organisation
3. Help the candidate understand the nature of the job and the expectations of the organisation to enable the candidate to make a decision on whether he or she will choose to work for the organisation

How do You Prepare for the Interview?

When your resume has been accepted by the organisation you applied to and you are invited for an interview, you should check your pre-interview to-do list to prepare yourself.

Research the company

You probably know a little something about your prospective employer by the time you make it to the interview stage. But now, it is important for you to obtain a good grasp of the company history, including its mission and vision and who the founders are, and that you are up-to-date on its latest news. Check the company's website and annual report (if available) to learn about the company's profile. Then do a Google News search to take a look at the company's social media profiles. Know how long the company has existed, the challenges faced, who its competitors are, and most important, what its problems are, especially those that hiring you would solve.

Investigate your role

Check the job title and find out what responsibilities typically go with that role. Assess your own experiences and how they would fit. Check salary surveys on such positions to determine the salary range. You need to know the minimum amount that you can accept so that you are asked to get into specifics, you can provide an acceptable answer. However, it is important to remain flexible as each company has its own salary range for each job. You can jeopardise your change of employment if you are too fixated on your salary expectation especially when you are just entering the job market.

Know who the key people are

If possible, find out the names of the people and their designations in the interview panel. If you are being interviewed by personnel outside of Human Resources, pay special attention to their background and experiences. Note any commonality with your background.

Prepare for common questions

Avoid giving canned answers to common interview questions by focusing on demonstrating how your skills, experiences, and passion can help the company to solve its problems. Assess your own strengths and weaknesses and remember your strong qualities rather than memorising pat replies to the questions.

Practise confident body language

Sit up straight, maintain eye contact with interviewers and shake hands firmly. In short, practice looking like someone who deserves to get the job.

Common Questions Asked by Interviewers

To gather more information about the candidate and to assess whether the candidate is a right fit for the job, interviewers tend to ask open-ended questions that may stress the candidate. Here are some common questions asked by interviewers.

1. Tell me more about yourself.
2. What are you most proud of?
3. Tell me about your strengths and weaknesses.
4. With your lack of relevant experiences, why should I employ you?
5. How good are you at coping in a crisis?
6. Who is your role model and why?
7. What things do you not like to do?
8. Why do you want to change your job?
9. Why do you want to work for us and how does this job position interest you?
10. What challenges are you looking for in this position?
11. Give us an example of a situation where you've faced conflict or difficult communication problems.
12. What would you like to be five years from now?
13. Tell me about a project or accomplishment that is most significant in your life so far.
14. We strive to make things better, faster, smarter or less expensive. We leverage technology or improve processes. In other words, we do more with less. Tell me a recent project that you have improved on resulting in greater efficiency and lower cost.
15. Please tell me an occasion in which you had to prioritise your work when working under pressure and tight deadlines.
16. What questions do you have for me?

Attending the Interview

When you attend an interview, pay attention to the following:

1. Arrive at the interview venue at least 25 minutes before the scheduled time given to you. This is to allow you to freshen up and to have time to complete the company's application form, if required.
2. Use perspirant to take care of body odour, if necessary. The same goes for bad breath. Be clean shaven and invest in a pair of leather shoes for the males.
3. Sleep early the night before and dress appropriately for the interview. This means no dangling jewellery, mini-skirt, sleeveless blouse, spaghetti

strap and sandles showing your toes, for the females. For the males, no gaudy ties, shorts, singlets instead of shirts, shiny belts, torn blue jeans and slippers instead of shoes.

4. Avoid having tattoos all over your body as some employers associate that with gang identity, and deem it inappropriate for their working environment.

5. Bring extra copies of your resume and education/work records and testimonial with you. This is especially useful when the interviewer is from another location and may not bring along your resume and other documents. Also, the company may want to make photocopies of your documents before or after the interview.

What You Should Avoid Saying during the Interview

Hiring managers/officers use the interview to gauge your fit for the job, your creativity, your ability to think on your feet, your emotional intelligence and your attitude. As such, it is important to remember that it is not what you say that counts. It is also how you say it – your tone of voice and body language will be watched closely as another indicator as to your overall fitness for the job at hand.

Never say the following:

1. "I am really nervous." No company wants to hire someone who lacks confidence.

2. "Let's talk money." Never discuss salary in the early stages of the interview. It may give the interviewer the wrong impression that you only care about money and not about aligning yourself to the mission and values of the company.

3. "I really need this job." — It gives the impression that you are desperate and this may indicate weakness. Your would-be employer is looking for someone who is seeking a long-term career, not merely a job.

4. "My current supervisor/employer is terrible." Never criticise the employer of your company. 'Even if the interviewer invites you to, never do it. It makes you sound bitter, negative and petty. It also shows that you could badmouth any boss or company in the future.

5. "I need …" Do not always talk about your needs. This is the time to talk about the needs of the company and how you can help to fulfil them. Talking only about your needs will flag you as someone who only cares for yourself and who is not a good team player.

6. "I love the benefits you offer." Do not bring up how much you love some of the company's benefits, such as the free snacks and recreation club. It only shows that you care more about the benefits than the company's success.

7. "I'd rather not say." Unless the interviewer asks you an inappropriate or discriminatory question, or something that makes you feel very uncomfortable, you should try to answer his or her queries. A job interview is never a time to play the "no comments" game. It will make you look unprepared or have something to hide.

8. "I do not have any questions for you" When asked whether you have any questions for the interviewer, never say "no". This makes you look unprepared for the interview, or worse, not interested in the company.

After the Interview

It is good practice to write a short thank-you note to your interviewer after the interview. Even if you are not selected for the post, you have created a good impression.

Conclusion

Both resume writing and performing at interviews are skills that can be improved and sharpened with practice. But you have to plan ahead and be prepared at all times. Nothing should be left to chance and you have to anticipate the questions that interviewers ask. You need to update your resume at all times to ensure that all information is accurate and up-to-date.

Chapter 15

Work Values Through Sports

John Tan

Desired work values can be cultivated through one's prior participation in sports or physical activity. The keywords are "can" and "cultivated". Sports itself is a vehicle to achieving varying goals. People indulge in sports for various reasons e.g., to win, to socialise and for health benefits. Sports involves more than just participating. It also entails spectating, and often by a huge audience. While engaging in the activity, participants may display desirable behaviours but at times, deplorable ones. For example, some well-reputed athletes have been noted for their honorable and charitable acts but also for some deplorable behaviours. Sports is often seen as a means to help develop character amongst young and impressionable individuals. Some feel that youths' involvement in sports should be accompanied by strict parental supervision or guidance.

Sports, essentially, can be perceived as a learning journey where new athletes, in developing into competent athletes, develop their character traits along the way. This "rite of passage" involves dealing with difficulties, decision making and facing the consequences of their actions. In general, sports provides a good rehearsal for life. Lessons can be learnt from winning or losing, and often such lessons are transferable to another area of one's life, including work life. Hence, instead of drifting along and enjoying the sporting experience, we should take better cognisance of the values that are acquired in the sporting arena, and adopt it for the workplace.

Setting Goals and Drawing Plans

The progression from a beginner sportsperson to a competent athlete involves planning. An athlete just does not get up in the morning and compete in the marathon race. He or she will have to determine the training required and put in the necessary preparations before being able to compete. It may take as long as six months just to be adequately prepared to complete a marathon run. One has to plan the training based on a year's timeline, breaking it up into phases and then refining it down to the daily training sessions. Often, the expertise of a coach is needed to assist in drawing up the necessary training plans and setting realistic goals and targets. Goals are specific standards of proficiency for a task and plans are actions mapped out to reach those goals (Gould, 1986). There may also be the need for training partners to provide company and motivation, and the necessary peer influence to adhere to plans. In the process, the young athlete learns to develop discipline through the training.

For a team sport, goals must be explicit, and are both individual- and team-specific. Setting goals entails individual technical details as well as tactical considerations when planning. Goals must not only be explicit, but they must also be realistic, so that expectations are managed and shared, whatever the results or outcome. Setting goals and planning provide both individuals and the team a clear direction to achieve the common and shared goals.

Likewise in working life, one will be more likely to succeed if there are goals and plans to achieve them. It is like a man driving a car — if he has a destination in his mind and a map to guide him; chances are that he will get there. Otherwise, it will be like what Bill Copeland, an author and poet, once said, "The trouble with not having a goal is that you can spend your life running up and down the field and never score."

Hard Work

One of the better values we learned in sports is hard work. A beginner in any sport will have to master some fundamental skills first. It could be hitting a shuttle in badminton, dribbling a basketball, kicking a football, etc. Although some of us are more natural in executing certain skills, there is no substitute for hard work in acquiring the skills required in sports. It is through hard work that one improves on one's skills, making up for the lack of natural athletic abilities and even optimising one's potential. For example, Laurentia Tan, The Straits Times' Athlete of the Year for 2012, developed cerebral palsy and profound deafness after birth. Doctors informed her parents that she would probably never walk. When she was in school, she fell so often and sustained so many minor injuries that her teachers and the school nurse affectionately nicknamed her "Trouble". She took up horse riding when she could hardly sit on the horse without two persons propping her upright (Singapore Sports Council, 2013). And through sheer hard work and giving up a job to train full time, she did us proud by winning four equestrian medals in two Paralympics. The value of hard work in sports is transferable to the work place. Regardless of the nature of the skill; be it welding or writing a software program, the more time we spent on it, the better we will get.

Discipline

There will always be distractions in our lives. It used to be television but now, surfing the Internet seems to be the top occupation for our deviating from what we set out to do. In sports, we need to learn and develop the required skills. Success does not come with just one good session. We usually have a training plan and a schedule to practice regularly. Most importantly, it is commitment to this schedule — keeping closely to the plan and shutting out all temptations and distractions. Occasionally, we may be discouraged with our progress, bored with the practice or even find the practice too draining, but without perseverance or persistence in keeping up with the training regime, the chance of success is greatly reduced. Even if victory is attained by "luck", it will not be as sweet as if you have toiled with unwavering discipline. For example, let us look at Dr Ben Tan's route to his Asian Games gold medal performance at Hiroshima in 1994. He shared that it was challenging to master the multi-dimensional skills in sailing. It took many years of consistent hard work to attain the results that he achieved (Singapore Sports Council, 2013). And through his competitive sailing years, he had to juggle his time between sailing and studies. So it was not just hard work but consistent and persistent hard work, which required discipline, that helped him reap his successes and victories. In the end he did not only get his gold medal in sailing but also a medical degree from the National University of Singapore.

The value of discipline in sports is indisputable — it is a necessary factor for success in the sporting field. The same discipline will reap success in the workplace and even help earn its possessor a reputation. Employers or clients in business value people who have the discipline to complete tasks. Sometimes they call it "good work ethics". If you can get yourself looked upon as a disciplined performer or one with good work ethics, you will be a valued person in your industry.

Along with discipline is patience. I am sure we are all familiar with the famous race between the tortoise and the hare — one of the stories in *Aesop's Fables*. The moral of the story is about how persistent hard work can overcome seemingly impossible feats. In this story, the tortoise could beat the hare in a running race. It is about knowing that it takes time to reach our goals even when the apparent odds are against us. We need to be patient and know our strengths and weaknesses, as it is important to work on our strengths and resolve our weaknesses. But plans alone, no matter how good they are, will not lead to anything without being carried out with patience and persistence.

Success comes with discipline, patience, perseverance and sheer hard work. Whether in sports or at work, success is often very satisfying. Former British Prime Minister Mrs Margaret Thatcher once said, "Look at a day when you are supremely satisfied at the end. It's not a day when you lounge around doing nothing; it's when you've had everything to do, and you've done it."

Relating to Others

In growing from a beginner to a competent athlete, one has to deal with other people in the process. There are the coaches, teammates and opponents. Practice sessions and competitions provide opportunities for interactions with different individuals. This enables us to learn to interact with others in order to achieve our goals, either in acquiring skills, in attaining our goals or in winning. We learn the importance of teamwork and leadership, and the social skills necessary to relate to our competitors.

In sports, we need coaches at both the beginning and high competitive levels. Coaches generally present themselves broadly as either autocratic or democratic mentors (Chelladurai, 1986). Their coaching styles, which may be a model to emulate, may depend on the circumstances of the task or the persons involved in the task.

The autocratic coaching style is commonly used in situations where a beginner in the sport needs to learn a specific technique efficiently. Such coaches will take full control of the session and carry out what is needed and the beginner is expected to follow instructions without asking questions. This coaching style — military-like and even business-like — is most commonly adopted in sports, in situations where there is little time given to achieve the task. The coach is deemed the most knowledgeable about the task. However, such coaches are often viewed as controlling and dictatorial, which often gives rise to resentment among their athletes. Athletes who have to follow such a coaching style would do well if they can learn how to follow the coach, be aware of the advantages of such a style, and draw the best out of the coach instead of being resentful. In working life our bosses can be autocratic too, so if one could learn from a similar coaching experience and deal positively with such a leader, goals can be achieved efficiently and with satisfaction.

On the other hand, democratic coaching styles invite the athletes to participate in the coaching process by encouraging them to adopt a "self-coaching" attitude. Such democratic coaching styles encourage a sense of accountability and involvement. Athletes with such coaches generally adapt quickly by being motivated in the learning process. Coaches who adopt such an approach can develop great relationships with their athletes. Compared to the autocratic approach, the democratic style generally yields less productive results and the process to achieving goals usually needs more time. Like the athletes who train under the democratic style, in the workplace, workers are more proactive and forthcoming with their inputs. Of course, athletes and workers would have to contend with the fact that at times directions may be less clear and therefore there may be a compromise in efficacy.

While engaging in sports, one also has the opportunity to relate with training mates or teammates. Teammates in sports are all working together to achieve the same sets of skills, playing by the same sets of rules and even partner each other like in a doubles game of badminton. There is a common point of interest and working towards a common goal. Bonding with teammates is relatively easy. There is no need to worry about making small talk in order to "break the ice"' after the game. There are plenty of things to share after a game like a fantastic goal, tough coach or rotten play. This "socialising" after the game usually continues on to after-game meetings and even parties, and these will extend one's social time. When asked to compare her schoolmates at Methodist Girls' School to those at the Sports School, Jazreel Tan (a member of the 2014 Asian Games women's bowling champion team) said that she "can talk more about sports with her classmates in sports school" (Muneerah, 2006).

With teammates there is a need to rely on each other for support in a game. You get to play off each other's strengths and defend each other's weaknesses. Such interactions inevitably build trust amongst each other. At times when your training mates struggle with a skill required, sharing a noteworthy observation or useful tip will go a long way towards building a sense of accomplishment and setting new heights in friendship.

When engaging in sports, there are rules to keep but more importantly, there are etiquettes to observe. There are unwritten friendly practices, like in golf, everyone present at the tee-box will keep silent and remain still when a fellow golfer makes a stroke. Observing etiquette in sports usually enhances friendship and respect; even with your rivals. One etiquette in sports is sportsmanship or gamesmanship — to show humility in winning and graciousness in losing. These will not only endear you to your teammates but also earn you admiration from your opponents.

As in sports, teamwork is essential in the work environment. Working as a team to gain victory or success is not an end by itself. Teamwork can also enrich our lives. Working selflessly, working for the team and not for ourselves alone, may help a team to achieve success. In sports, taking pride in being a cohesive team and relying on one another for support to achieve the common target can certainly provide greater satisfaction than actually scoring the goal itself. At the workplace, standing up for a colleague and knowing that your colleague will defend you at any cost is a joy and comfort that anyone would treasure.

Dr Ben Tan illustrated the importance of teamwork when he explained that in sailing, even in a one-boat sailing event, it requires cohesive teamwork with sparring partners and coaches. He also related the value of teamwork in his role as a doctor when he said, "I am useless without the team, as I only diagnose. It is the physiotherapists, podiatrists and others who actually deliver the treatment." (Singapore Sports Council, 2013).

Teamwork is also important in any corporate organization, big or small. Keppel FELS Senior Engineer Daryl Tai said that in the working environment, it is about managing people and knowing when and what approaches to use for different individuals and for different circumstances (Teo, 2012).

Overcoming Adversity

Athletes usually experience adversity at some time in their sporting careers, but it is the ones who learn how to overcome adversity who achieves the highest levels in sports.

Take Karoly Takacs, who was a sergeant in the Hungarian army. He was then one of the best pistol shooters in the world and widely tipped to win the gold in the 1936 Olympic Games. But he was not allowed to compete in that Olympic Games because he was not a commissioned officer. Subsequently, the rule changed to allow non-commissioned officers to participate in the later Olympics. Unfortunately for him, the 1940 and 1944 Olympics were cancelled because of the Second World War. The worst blow for him was during an army training session, when a hand grenade exploded in his hand. The explosion blew away his right hand. Did the explosion also blow away his Olympic gold medal winning aspiration? No, within a month, Karoly was back on the shooting range, learning to shoot with his left hand. Karoly went on to win gold medals in the 1948 and 1952 Olympic Games, shooting with his left hand.

Prakash Iyer in his book *The Habit of Winning* said, "We all have moments in our lives when we seem so close to glory, but suddenly lose everything. Our dreams get shattered. We feel vanquished, crushed, beaten and defeated. When that happens, think of Karoly. In fact, think like him." (Iyer, 2012).

In sporting competitions, there is only winning or losing, success or failure. In a race or competition amongst many teams or individuals, there can only be one champion or winner. So the chance of experiencing defeat is relatively high. Many athletes tend to dwell on their mistakes and failures. How do they get back up in their sport again? Most get to see a bigger perspective or a longer-term perspective that there is always another game, the next race or match. The loss or defeat is only a little setback meant for a lesson to be learnt and build on, en route to greater victory later on. Defeat is meant to motivate one to work harder, not to give up.

Life in our workplace may not be fair; there are setbacks and other adversities that may occur, just like in sports. At times when we encounter failure or defeat, we must learn to accept it but not with resignation. It must be with the humility that we will get more organised and work much harder in order to attain that elusive goal. It is said that Thomas Edison made over 1,000 unsuccessful attempts before he finally invented the light bulb. Overcoming adversity or setbacks is a skill and a value that we often learn in sports, and it will serve us well in our working lives as well.

Conclusion

Sports is sometimes seen as a rehearsal for one's work life. In sport, you learn a skill; you learn how to work with your teammates; you go for a competition; you win or you lose. If you win, you celebrate and if you lose, you pick yourself up and work harder and then you compete again. If you do not make your living through sporting competitions, the winning or losing will have few consequences for you. But certainly if you pick the positive values that you have learned from participating in sports, and then apply these to your work life, you will have a head start over others.

So if we view sports participation as a learning journey and take note of the lessons, work values can indeed be cultivated through sports. Besides instilling values, sports can also enrich your work life in other ways. Sports participation can enhance your physique, improve your health and increase your work capacity. If you have not already engaged in sports on a regular basis, you should start now!

References

Chelladurai, P. (1986). Styles of decision making in coaching. In Williams, J.M. (ed.), *Applied Sports Psychology: Personal Growth to Peak Performance*. Palo Alto, CA: Mayfield Publishing. 107–1118.

Gould, D. (1986). Goal setting for peak performance. In Williams, J.M. (ed.), *Applied Sports Psychology: Personal Growth to Peak Performance*. Palo Alto, CA: Mayfield Publishing. 133–147.

Iyer, P. (2012). *The Habit of Winning*. India: Penguin Books.

Muneerah, (2006). A subtle striking star. In Phoon, K.H. (ed.). A Fledgling Sporting Singapore: Stories of Singapore Young Sports Talents. Singapore: Candid Creation Publishing. 207–220.

Singapore Sports Council (2013). *Game for Life: Lives Made Extraordinary through Sport.* Singapore Sports Council Singapore.

Teo, J (2012). Using sports values in the workplace. *The Straits Times,*13 February 2012.

Chapter 16

Preparing Our Children
for Tomorrow's World

Tan Khye Suan

As loving parents, we all hope to see our children grow up prepared for the challenges of tomorrow's world. We know how daunting adult life can be, with challenges thrown every day at us. We hope that our children will not only survive these challenges, but also rise above them and be counted as people of worth in society.

Hence, we need to get our children ready for the world they will face in the future. But the world is ever-changing and the challenges we face today are not likely to be those that they will face in their time. We will not be there to help them along. They will have to face the challenges on their own. How then can we prepare our children for their world of tomorrow?

Very often, parents think that in order for their children to be able to take on the challenges of tomorrow's world, they need the best education, the right qualifications, the right career, and reasonable wealth as well as status. All these are reasonable goals, but, to face the world of tomorrow, they should also be taught age-old values. I believe that parents should impart to their children qualities of independence, confidence, resilience and moral values. These will help our children face life's challenges.

One great concern that parents have is how children will cope with their working life. How we raise our children will have a huge impact in determining how they will perform as working adults in future.

Employers will always want to see their employees being able to work independently as soon as possible, with minimum "hand-holding". In the eyes of employers, the ability to work independently is equated to productivity. A good employee is also able to take instructions well, receive feedback constructively and is teachable.

All employers want employees with integrity. When an employee has integrity, he is trustworthy. This makes it easier for employers to entrust the employee with responsibilities. No employer wants to employ someone that cannot be trusted. Coupled with integrity is responsible decision making. When a person has integrity, it is quite reasonable to expect that this person will make decisions responsibly, whether the decision is for himself, his family members or his employer.

It is important that parents should focus not just on the paper chase but on instilling qualities like independence and integrity that will bring respect for their children and honour to their parents.

Proper Guidance towards Independence

Generally, I see two broad categories of parents whose approaches to parenting are not helpful in preparing their children to become independent adults. The first category of parents cannot let go of their children. The second category of parents let go of their children too quickly.

The first category of parents struggles with the idea of granting independence to their children, especially when they become teenagers. (Adolescence is the period of transition from childhood to adulthood. Henceforth, reference will mostly be made to teenager/teenagers rather than child/children, as much work in guidance usually occurs during adolescence.) These parents are often plagued by the fear that their teenager will not be able to make it without their help, and tend to be over-protective. Hence, their teenager is given very little opportunities to learn how to make good decisions. As a result, the teenager becomes dependent on parents, lacking self-confidence, initiative and resilience. He or she may also have problem developing healthy relationships with friends and persons of the opposite gender. A strong-willed teenager may experience a lot of conflicts with his parents as he or she fights for independence. Conversely, parents of a strong-willed teenager may experience a lot of anger and frustration when their teenager rebels against them.

The second category of parents, at some stage of their teenager's life, is likely to revoke the independence that they have granted so quickly. Without proper guidance, the teenager does not know how to make good decisions, especially on emotional, social and moral issues. As a result, the teenager may likely make poor decisions that result in repercussions that his or her parents did not anticipate. These may include emotional distress, anti-social behaviour; and, for some, brushes with the law. For a teenager who is timid and less assertive, that teenager may become insecure, lacking in confidence and self-esteem. The teenager may also become victims of bullies.

To help teenagers learn to become independent adults, parents must consciously give them appropriate opportunities to learn how to make good decisions. For a start, allow teenagers, in early adolescence, to take baby steps to learn how to make decisions on not-so-important matters. As teenagers demonstrate their ability and confidence in making good decisions on the not-so-important matters, they should be allowed to graduate to making decisions on more important matters.

A good platform for teenagers to practice good decision making is self-management. Self-management is a battleground on which many teenagers and parents have fought. When fought unwisely, both parents and teenagers will come out of the battleground badly scarred and resentful of each other. Yet, this is the best platform for learning good decision making and independence. Areas for teenagers to self-manage include deciding on the clothes they want to wear for various occasions, the food they choose to eat, the time they spend on studies and with their friends and the co-curricular activities (CCA) they participate in. These are safe areas and with consistent engagement by parents, teenagers can be gently guided to make the right choices.

When teenagers make appropriate choices, parents should praise them. Give reasons why the choice is a good one. If an unwise choice is made, parents should explain why the choice is not a good one. However, parents should also allow teenagers some room for differences in opinions, ideas and choices.

The reason for unhappy outcomes occur when parents adopt the "win-lose" mindset when guiding teenagers. Parents tend to feel strongly that they must get their way and the teenager must comply after parents have given their views. Such a mindset will not help achieve the objective of training teenagers towards good decision making, independence and confidence, even in the "safe haven" of simple self-management. Usually, teenagers do take the views of their parents seriously. However, they must be given time to accept our views; they must feel that in fact, *they* are in control and that they themselves have made the choice to abide by their parents' views.

It has to be reiterated that parents must change their mindset. They must allow teenagers some room for making mistakes within tolerable boundaries. Parents should not react adversely towards mistakes and less ideal choices and decisions made by teenagers. By helping teenagers to make wise decisions in small things, we train them to make wise decisions on more important things in future. So, by gently reviewing with the teenager their decisions and the corresponding outcomes, parents can **coach** their teenager towards independence and confidence in decision making.

A Coaching Relationship

The word "coach" has been used a couple of times already. Perhaps, at this point, it is best to give an idea of what coaching is.

Let us think of a coach who is guiding a footballer. The coach must determine the footballer's strength and limitation. The coach must determine if the footballer has the potential to be a defender, a striker, a midfielder, a winger or a goalkeeper. If the footballer has strengths as a good defender, a coach will never try to train that footballer to become a striker. It is, at best, a poor fit. Having identified the strengths of the footballer, the coach will then proceed to build the footballer based on his strengths.

For the footballer to perform well, he must trust his coach. The footballer must believe and accept that the coach has his interest at heart and intends to develop him to his fullest potential. For the footballer to perform well, he must then accept instructions from his coach and act according to instructions.

When the footballer is fielded for a match, the coach must believe that he can perform up to the expected standard. The coach will always review the footballer's performance after each match. When the footballer does well, the coach will highlight the high points of the footballer's performance and encourage him to continue with higher levels of performance. There will be times when the footballer does not meet the coach's expectations. However, the coach will not be punitive and axe the footballer from the team immediately. Usually, the coach will help the footballer to identify his weaknesses. He will also help the footballer find ways to overcome his weaknesses. The coach may also provide some tips on how to do better.

It is best that such a coaching relationship between parents and children is strongly established as early as possible, even before children reach adolescence. The coaching approach is probably the best way for parents to work with children, especially as teenagers.

Building Confidence and Resilience

Parents must have an open channel of communication to work closely with teenagers. A strong trusting relationship (like that between the example above of a coach and a footballer) must exist between parents and teenagers. In that way, teenagers will be able to appreciate, understand and accept willingly that what their parents seek to impart to them is all for their well-being.

Scolding, nagging and repetitive demands for compliance from our children will not help, especially when they are teenagers. These actions tend to reinforce the perception that we, as parents, do not trust them. Hence, parents need to use positive approaches, focusing on their teenagers' strengths (e.g., talents, inclinations and interests) and continually encouraging them.

Very often, teenagers find it hard to trust and work with their parents because parents tend to emphasise teenagers' weaknesses. It is not wrong to highlight weaknesses, but dwelling on weaknesses only serve to discourage teenagers. If teenagers are constantly told of their weaknesses, they will be discouraged and lose confidence in themselves. Eventually, they become disillusioned and lose the ability to be resilient.

By focusing on teenagers' strengths, parents will be able to build confidence and resilience in teenagers, even when there are setbacks. With positive encouragement and support from parents, teenagers can perform well in their strength areas; first achieving small successes, then greater successes. The constant progression of successes is important to help teenagers develop confidence and resilience.

It will be good for parents to remember the time when their teenagers were infants becoming toddlers. Remember the time they were learning how to walk? As parents, did we not hold their hands so that they could learn to take their first steps? After some training, did we not let go so they could try walking on their own? They take a step or two. Then they fall. Did we not encourage them with words like "Never mind the fall, get up and try again." Were we not coaches to our children when they were very young? Did we not give our children confidence and resilience? And, because we gave them confidence and resilience, our children grew up having the ability to walk instead of continuing to crawl! As parents, we should continue to do the same thing as we did when our children were young so that they can become independent, confident and resilient.

In the process of preparing our children for tomorrow's world, parents must be aware of a common pitfall. More often than not, parents tend to live their own dreams in their teenager. Parents may be placing teenagers under undue demands and pressures, pushing them into areas that they are not strong in. As a result, they may not be able to achieve the goals set out by their parents. This will cause them to lose confidence and resilience. Teenagers are likely to be resentful of their parents while parents become disappointed with their teenagers.

Right Moral Values: The Basis for Making Decisions

Good and wise decisions are always made based on a set of moral values that a person adopts. These moral values are usually tried and tested, and are, at least, the basic accepted norms of society. Usually moral values are also influenced by personal or religious beliefs. But we should focus on one important value: integrity.

Integrity is about choosing to deal with things truthfully, choosing to deal with people justly, and choosing to do the right thing regardless of the situation. In any walk of life, integrity is valued far more than qualifications. I have seen people being passed over for promotion or dismissed from their jobs because of their lack of integrity. I have seen people being respected because of integrity.

It may surprise parents to know that teenagers have a strong sense of integrity. They usually start out in adolescence subconsciously supporting the values of truth, justice and right actions. Have you heard your teenagers demanding to know the truth in one situation or another, asking for fairness in treatment for themselves or their friends, or insisting that they are doing the right thing against the grain of situations or circumstances? The strong sense of integrity in teenagers should be encouraged and not worn down. We should be teaching teenagers how to apply integrity wisely.

Our children learn the right moral values by watching us in action, not by being taught by us. Very often, we see ourselves choosing to tell white lies because it is more convenient to do so or choosing decisions that will attract the least objections. Our teenagers will be very quick to sieve out our actions and see us as hypocrites. Then when we try to teach them moral values, they will challenge us. As parents, we need to walk the talk.

As parents, we have a set of moral values that we want to impart to our teenagers. Some parents may not be satisfied just to pass on a set of moral values to their teenagers. They want to pass on their personal and religious beliefs on which their value system is built upon. The passing on of their value system and religious beliefs is an area of great struggle that many parents experience with their teenagers.

For teenagers to be able to accept their parents' value system and even religious beliefs, teenagers have to be convinced that their parents truly believe and live by these values and beliefs. Teenagers must see that parents are practising what they preach. Very often, parents are very didactic in approach as they try to get their teenagers to accept their value system and beliefs. Being preachy will not motivate teenagers to want to adopt their parents' value system or religious beliefs. The best way is for parents to practise what they preach. Teenagers are only convinced by the congruence of their parents' words and actions.

Hence, the best way to impart to your teenager the basis of good decision making is to show them by example. Parents will have to show teenagers how their value system and religious beliefs work in their own lives before teenagers are convinced to do the same.

Gradual Release towards Independence

Parents should start the process of giving gradual freedom of decision making as early as possible to teenagers. This is because in their early teenage years, teenagers may still be malleable. This will lead to the gradual building of trust by parents towards their teenagers and, thereby, confidence in their teenagers' ability to manage themselves. As trust and confidence are built up, more freedom and bigger issues can be given to the teenager to manage.

Parents should not start their teenager off with decision making on big issues. Remember that the key word is **gradual**. Parents should start their teenager off with very small issues like the choice of appropriate clothes to wear on a family gathering. Parents can then proceed to let teenagers self-manage on matters like how they go to school, return home from school, or go to a school activity on their own. The issues can gradually become bigger, like going out to a movie with friends, or attending a friend's birthday party. If the gradual release is successful, as time goes by, autonomy can eventually be given to teenagers on big decisions like their further education and career choice.

This process is the same as a driving instructor teaching his trainee how to drive. The trainee starts off with the basics like starting the engine, engaging the gear and moving the car off from a stationary position. All these are learnt in the confines of the driving circuit. As the trainee masters the basics, the instructor will impart more complex skills to the trainee. Remember that throughout the training, the trainee is the person handling the car. Not the instructor. Although the instructor has facilities to intervene when the trainee makes wrong moves, he usually refrains from doing so, if the mistakes are not major or life-threatening. Similarly, as parents allow the teenager to take the driver's seat, remember to allow for some mistakes to be made within certain reasonable boundaries.

Parents may be wondering why the recommendation is for them to allow the process of gradual release to start as early as possible for their teenagers. This is because teenagers need time to learn. Teenagers do not grow up overnight. The earlier parents start working with their teenagers, the more time the parents have to coach and guide them. A longer runway for teenagers to take off into adulthood is safer than a short runway. A short runway has less room for mistakes.

With such a gradual release, I believe our children will be able to face the challenges of tomorrow.

Chapter 17

Preparing Future-Ready Students: A Teacher's Perspective

Brian Lui

Introduction

I love T-shirts! They are comfortable, fun to wear and have many quirky messages printed on them. I chanced upon one such T-shirt while shopping, with a paradoxical statement printed on the front. "The Future isn't what it used to be".

It was an amusing message but it is also a stark reality check for educators in today's fast-changing world. If we do not know what the world will look like in ten years' time, how will we know what to teach our students to prepare them for their lives?

Our quest for academic excellence borders on being "frantic" as can be seen from how many parents strive to get their children a head start in life, and provide their children with tuition and enrichment courses to supplement their school studies. However, whilst good results indeed open doors for students, do they guarantee success in the future? Is there something else missing?

Something is Missing

Although we might not know what the future holds for our next generation of workers, we still can look at trends today to get some kind of idea of the current employment market. In 2013, the Guardian Online published findings from a study of more than 500,000 advertisements by the search company Adzuna. It revealed that the ten words and phrases most commonly used by UK employers to describe the type of person they were looking for were

1. Organised
2. Communication skills
3. Motivated
4. Qualified
5. Flexible
6. Degree
7. Commitment
8. Passionate
9. Track record
10. Innovative

What is interesting to me is that the top three have nothing to do with academics. In fact, qualifications and a degree feature in fourth and sixth place, respectively, while having a track record comes in only at ninth place.

So, what can we conclude from the work requirements of today's employers? What does this all mean for someone just finishing school and is entering the workforce for the first time? I think there is a lot to learn.

Firstly, good academic results are not enough to prepare students for today's future, let alone tomorrow's future. Therefore, we should not look at grades as the only valuable outcome from our school days as there are so many more rich lessons to bring way with us. Next, the good news for a new job entrant is that having a track record isn't as important as having qualities like being organised, having communication skills or being motivated and flexible. Therefore, you would do well to strengthen your abilities in these areas.

From Adzuna's findings, it would seem that the workers of tomorrow need to navigate through a volatile, uncertain, complex and ambiguous future if they are to remain relevant and if they are to thrive. For example, to do well in your career, you would have to successfully juggle and prioritise a lot of work thrown at you (organised). You will be required to be articulate and clear, and show that you can work with and handle people (communication skills). You are going to have to work independently and often find and work on your own tasks as well as be flexible enough to take on others here and there (motivated/flexible/passionate). You will need to think of novel ways to get through the issues and challenges you're going to face (innovative). You'll be expected to work long hours and do less enjoyable things when necessary, and despite all this, be committed to the organisation and stay for the long haul (commitment).

In fact, this is exactly how students need to apply themselves to be successful in their studies and in school. In short, these traits are actually learnt as students!

All of us have experienced trying to cope with studying for subjects that we're not so good at, subjects that we dread and struggle with. Struggling through and overcoming setbacks in studies teaches us courage, commitment, resilience, patience and determination. Overcoming setbacks gives us confidence to try harder and take on bigger challenges. Juggling numerous subjects and other school responsibilities teaches us to focus, prioritise and manage our time. And even if we are doing well in some subjects, working towards even better grades instead of settling for a lower grade teaches us the value of excellence.

Sadly, however, I find that today's students are so accustomed to what I call the "instant noodles" syndrome, where they want things "now". Perhaps it is partially the result of technology and the Internet allowing us to access everything immediately at the press of an enter key. This is a worrying trend which, in my honest opinion, can only be balanced out by giving students programmes and experiences to develop these employability traits.

I believe that future-ready students need this foundation and more, to have confidence in themselves, to be resilient in the face of difficulties and uncertainty. They need to be lifelong learners, self-directed in their learning, and creative and resourceful. They need to be contributing members of something bigger than themselves, to show care and concern for others and actively work for the greater good.

The Ministry of Education (MOE) succinctly describes all these as desired student outcomes (DSO): confident person, self-directed learner, active contributor and concerned citizen. In schools, we address the development of DSO through the three purposes of schooling: vocation, personal formation and socialisation.

We Begin with a Problem

Whilst there are many ways to achieve the purposes, I believe that that best answer lies in a problem. Let me explain using an example from a design and technology class.

Teacher A tells his students, "This is a hammer, and it is used to knock nails. This is a screwdriver and we use it with screws. This is a saw, which we use to saw wood. Now let's make a wooden toy car."

Teacher B tells her students, "Hey, today we've got an exciting lesson. We're going to make a wooden toy car! Now, how shall we go about doing this?"

What is the difference between Teacher A and Teacher B? Teacher A tells his students what they need to know, how to use the tools and then assigns them the task. Teacher B poses a problem for the student, where they need to identify what they need to know and then learn and apply the information to solve the problem.

Teacher A has used a traditional learning method. Teacher B has used problem-based learning (PBL). PBL forces the students out of their comfort zones and to find their own solutions to problems individually or as teams. PBL aims to help students develop flexible knowledge, effective problem-solving skills, self-directed learning, effective collaboration skills and intrinsic motivation. PBL address the vocation part of the purpose of schooling. Vocation implies students' development in the literacy and numeracy competencies, as well as in the 21st century skills required for thriving in tomorrow's workforce. But what about the areas of personal formation and socialisation?

The Case for Character

In 2010, I was the Head of Department of Character and Citizenship Education (CCE). In one of the CCE department meetings, I asked the teachers, "Hypothetically, would you rather your own children be (1) academically excellent but void of good character, or (2) of good character but average academically?" They all chose (2). I smiled and said, "then we should wish the same for our students. We must teach character."

By teaching character, we also address students' personal formation and social growth. Personal formation means students being grounded in good values and having self-awareness and self-management. Socialisation allows students to gain greater social awareness of things happening around them and to manage relationships in these contexts.

Through schooling, children develop the following three aspects of character:

1. Performance character
2. Moral character
3. Social character

Dr Thomas Lickona describes performance character as consisting of character strengths such as self-discipline and best effort that enable us to pursue our personal best. He also describes moral character as knowing, valuing and doing the right thing. Dr Sharon Stoll describes social character as consisting of values such as loyalty, dedication, sacrifice, teamwork and good citizenship, important values to have when a person navigates through a social setting.

Indeed, from the study conducted by Adzuna, apart from qualifications, a degree and a track record, the other seven words can be subsumed under two of the three as follows:

Performance Character: Organised, Motivated, Flexible, Commitment, Passionate and Innovative

Social Character: Communication Skills

But what of moral character? Aren't moral values required in a work environment?

Consider the following argument. A person with a strong social character may have little or no moral character. Similarly for performance character, a person might be a focused and resilient individual but lacks integrity in his or her life. Think about the difference between former US President Dwight Eisenhower and the former dictator of Nazi Germany, Adolf Hitler. Both brilliant and capable men; both served in the military in World War 2; both lead their countries; but what a world of difference a lack of morality makes!

Likewise, imagine a capable employee who chooses not to do his best, or is perpetually late, or sabotages his colleague to cover up his own error. If you were an employer, would you want such a person in your organisation?

Character education is therefore a critical prerequisite for employability skills. Values like integrity and honesty, sincerity and patience are fundamental building blocks for employment.

In my quest to understand what shapes character, I stumbled upon an ethics toolkit on the Internet designed by the New Zealand Immigration Advisors Authority. They created this training document for its members, in which it states that

- a person's beliefs shape his values
- a person's values shape his attitudes
- a person's attitudes shape his behaviour

And we all know that behaviour over time shapes character.

The idea of shaping a student's character thus implies that personal formation and socialisation are addressed through his or her beliefs, values, attitudes and behaviour in a social context.

Valuing Values

Think about the following questions for a moment: Does good behaviour imply good values? Could it be possible for a student to exhibit good behaviour without having good values relating to that behaviour?

Consider this scenario. A boy has the intention of tossing a piece of tissue paper on the floor. Before he can do so, he sees his teacher walking towards him and decides to throw it into the bin instead. Did the boy exhibit the right behaviour? Yes. Did the boy have the right values to begin with? No.

My point is that consistent good behaviour only happens when people have embraced good values and a good foundation of social emotional (SE) competencies, which over time, lead to good character. However, how do we develop character, exactly?

Putting values in action develops character. It is as simple as that! This definition comes from the social and emotional learning (SEL) package for schools published in 2008. It implies that if we are to shape children's character, we must begin by shaping their values.

Putting Values into Action

Apart from character traits like resilience and focus, it is difficult for other facets of character to be taught when a student is sitting behind a desk. Indeed, if social and emotional competencies are to be learnt, students have to do so in social settings. This is where the full spectrum of SEL can take place — self-awareness, self-management, social awareness, relationship management and responsible decision making — all grounded on sound core values.

These social settings need to be created, and hence there is a need for values in action (VIA) experiences. These experiences are very different from the community involvement programmes (CIP) of the past. The difference is in the focus. Well-crafted VIA experiences engage students' "heads, hearts and hands" i.e., cognitively, affectively and physically.

Take for example two different students given the experience of cleaning a beach. For the first student, he was simply taken to the beach by his teacher, given a trash bag and told to pick up as much litter as possible. At the end of the activity he might say, "The beach was dirty. I picked up so much litter. I'm tired."

Now, imagine that for the second student, his teacher gives him the task of researching how litter impacts the ecosystem. In the course of his research, he learnt about where this litter was coming from. He also researched on how many tonnes of litter Singapore generates in a day. The actual litter picking then follows this, after which the teacher sits the class down to discuss what they saw, how it made them feel, what they discovered and eventually how they could grow from this experience. This then motivates the student to start a school campaign to get fellow students to reduce-reuse-recycle.

What makes the second student's learning richer? It is the elements of PBL, where the student is posed a problem and he needs to identify what he needs to know and then learn and apply the information to solve the problem.

Rich Learning Requires the "Eureka" Moment

Memories and experiences colour our world and give meaning to our lives. Some of the most memorable moments of my life are the birth of my children and the first time I completed running a marathon. What makes these moments and experiences significant are the positive emotions attached to them. Significant moments and experiences of learning have a similar effect.

"Eureka!", the expression made famous by the Greek mathematician Archimedes, signifies the triumphant discovery of something. In the same manner, we need to create "Eureka!" moments of learning for students through authentic SEL experiences. These moments happen when students navigate themselves though challenging experiences and emerge with positive emotions attached to the learning. These experiences are characterised by dissonance that forces students to reflect on their own value system, whilst taking them out of their comfort zone. Learning moments of this nature are truly significant, with many making turning points in people's lives.

Creating Learning Moments

There are many daily learning moments that can be harnessed to teach students SE competencies. However, greater impact is generated when these learning moments are created instead; where we can control what values and SE competencies students will learn.

The challenge is how to create these learning moments in a VIA activity. This is my personal formula.

Choose the learning outcomes

Which values and SE competencies do you wish to teach? This is the most important question. It determines how any experience will be shaped to distil the learning.

Take for example the beach-cleaning experience. If you wanted to expound on the value of resilience, and the SE domain of relationship management, you could focus your questions on the experience of going through difficult situations as a group and how the group communicated with each other during the process. If you wanted to focus on the value of respect and the SE domain of self-awareness, then you might use questions pertaining to preserving the environment for others and our level of active citizenry.

I offer a word of caution, though. If we try to focus on too many things at once, we might end up with nothing in the end, as we risk students not having explored deeply enough for each SE competency.

Choose the platform

Is the experience at a class or CCA level? Are you going to incorporate the learning into a cohort-level overseas trip?

The platform you choose will greatly determine the involvement level of each student. The more students there are in the activity, the less likely each student will be challenged to work outside of their comfort zones. For any given activity, smaller groups mean that each member has to pull his or her own weight to move the group forward. Greater dissonance can be generated in smaller groups.

Choose the experience

There are so many kinds of experiences students can embark on. The following lists a few:

- Paint over graffiti
- Plan a drug-free club for the school
- Create a public service announcement (PSA)
- Produce an anti-crime or anti-drug or anti-violence play and perform it for others
- Create and distribute a list of hotlines or agency links for teenagers who might need help

I've found some good places on the Internet to find meaningful activities for VIA. Here are two you could start with.

- http://learningtogive.org/
- http://128.121.178.253/SERVICE/webresources.html

What is important to note is that regardless of the experiences selected, a creative teacher can create many different learning outcomes as with the beach-cleaning example.

It is also important to consider whether students have an interest for the activity in the first place. This ensures that there will be a high level of engagement. This does not mean that the experience needs to be fun. It means that students have something that catches their interest. They may also like the fact that they are spending time with their friends despite doing an activity that takes them out of their comfort zone.

Create the reflective tasks and questions

I think that good reflective tasks and questions help teachers to do two things.

Firstly, they help frame the learning. For example, if you were taking students to Vietnam to do a VIA activity, preparing them before a trip with research tasks about the language, people, culture, history and economy of the country will help to deepen students' appreciation of the trip they are about to embark on. This will make the trip more meaningful and deepen students' learning from their overseas experience. We would kill the spirit of VIA if students were simply tourists, with an itinerary of two days of shopping and only half a day of service to the community.

Secondly, good questions also give students handles with which they can better reflect on their experiences. The Experiential Learning Model (Kolb, 1984) provides excellent scaffolding for students to distil learning from their experiences. This cyclic model consists of four stages: (1) Concrete experience or "Do", (2) Reflective observation or "Observe", (3) Abstract conceptualisation or "Think" and (4) Active experimentation or "Plan". The experience that you craft represents the "Do" stage. However, in my opinion, it is more important how they learn from the experience and hence, stages (2)–(4) should be planned and executed well.

Personally, I prefer using simple words for my students when I tackle stages (2)–(4). I use four key action words: See, Feel, Discover and Grow. The questions look like this:

From the experience,

1. What did you SEE?
2. How did that make you FEEL?
3. What have you DISCOVERED about others or about yourself?
4. How can you GROW from this experience?

There are other types of questions I like to use to extend students learning based on the selected learning outcomes. For example, in my school's overseas trip we have global citizenship as one of our learning outcomes. Some questions pertaining to this include the following:

1. While we are visitors to another country, what are our responsibilities

   - to Singapore
   - to the country of our visit
   - to the environment
   - to the world

2. Even though we are all teenagers, can we really make a difference? Why? How?

Character: Taught or Caught?

One important question to ask ourselves is whether character is taught or caught. I think the answer is a combination of both.

Character is taught

I remember a true story of one student who had a temper management issue. This particular day, his temper had flared again and he got into a quarrel with another student. Consequently, he was sent to the general office for a "time-out". Before long, his Form Teacher came by and started shouting at him, saying "How many times must I tell you to control your temper?" I stopped literally in my tracks.

It is easy to tell a child what he should be doing right, but aren't we supposed to guide him how to do it right? I think this is something we as teachers need to reflect on. We teach, we don't just tell.

For this boy, this could have been an excellent learning moment. If the teacher had sat him down and helped him through his anger issues, he would have learnt much more: how to identify his anger triggers, strategies to prevent his anger from flaring; how to communicate his frustrations in a more positive manner. However, the learning moment was lost.

As with the teaching of all other subjects, another important thing to note is that the quality of students' learning is directly impacted by the quality of the teacher's teaching. Along with our daily duties, we must make the effort to continuously grow as teachers: in curriculum design, pedagogy and assessment. There will always be better ways to do things, better ways to craft lessons, better ways to deliver the lesson and better ways to carry out formal and informal assessments.

Character is caught

Students learn quickly from watching others which makes imitation a key medium for learning, from toddlers playing *masak-masak* (toys) to teenagers walking like their favourite popstars.

This brings me to two points; firstly, role-modelling. It is critical that we consistently role-model good behaviour. Remember the story of the boy with the temper management issue? Remember his Form Teacher shouting at him? How can we expect students to learn to manage their temper when we ourselves cannot manage ours? However, if we show patience and kindness, we can then speak with authority about patience and kindness, and our students will quickly catch these.

Secondly, peer pressure, which is a powerful tool. Imagine a teacher sitting an entire class down to discuss a bullying incident that happened between two students. Imagine the teacher asking each student one at a time to share his or her feelings and opinions. Imagine the positive impact on the victim. Also imagine how the bully would feel. My guess is that the positive peer pressure would have a positive impact on everyone and each student in the discussion would have grown firmer in his or her conviction about anti-bullying.

Have Students Learnt?

I believe that teaching isn't teaching if learning did not take place. I have already discussed how quality teaching is key to students' learning. In addition to this, there is another important piece in this puzzle: assessment.

There are many modes of formal and informal assessment modes that teachers can use to check if students have learnt. For example, for formal assessment, teachers can use surveys, reflection journals, worksheets and even written peer-assessment tasks. Here is a simple 3-2-1 written activity that I use for my overseas school trips.

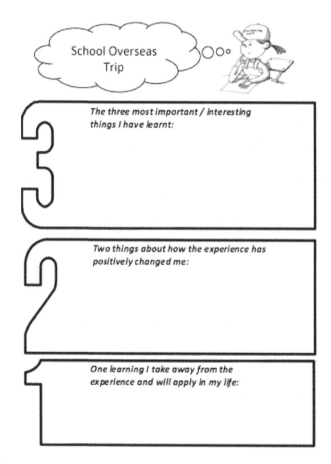

Informal assessment modes give teachers the opportunity to observe students in action and give timely feedback, clarify misconceptions early, affirm students' positive contributions or give interventive support if necessary. Informal assessment can be more fun as well. For example, teachers can step back and watch students conducting the VIA activity and step in if needed. During the post-activity segment, activities like circle time give teachers the chance to listen to students and use peer influence to reinforce learning too. There are many ways informal assessment can be carried out. My thoughts about this are that we should be creative and have fun crafting and implementing them.

My Final Thoughts

Creating future-ready students requires the three purposes of schooling to be achieved (vocation, personal formation, socialisation) to deliver the desired student outcomes (confident person, self-directed learner, active contributor and concerned citizen). Character development is key — it strengthens students' performance and moral and social character traits which are critical requisite skill sets and traits for employability.

Creating future-ready students also means that we must address the development of students' cognitive and affective domains together. Creating good values in action experiences will go a long way to helping students learn and grow to their fullest potential. The use of the problem-based learning approach in a social setting creates powerful experiences for our students.

Such programmes and experiences, however, should not be "one-off" in nature. As with other areas of learning, regular practice is crucial for success. When we activate their "head, heart and hands" regularly enough in the learning process, students begin to form good habits and will be well on their way to being future-ready.

As I write this, I'm conscious that these paragraphs are only my personal perspective. Through the process of writing this, I've also reflected deeply and have learnt greatly from this experience. I am grateful for this opportunity and I hope that you have found some useful ideas that you can use to prepare yourself or others to be future-ready.

References

Immigration Advisors Authority, New Zealand Government (2013). *Ethics Toolkit.* Retrieved on 23 April 2015 from http://www.iaa.govt.nz/advisor/ ethics-toolkit/

Kolb, D. A. (1984). *Experiential Learning: Experience as the Source of Learning and Development.* Englewood Cliffs, NJ: Prentice-Hall.

Chapter 18

Nurturing Primary Students for the Real World

Siah Siew Ling & Chiok Hwee Fen

The start of a brand new year brings about a great surge of emotions for everybody in schools. All teachers and students are eager to see how the year unfolds. Teachers and educators want to teach well and plan engaging and enriching lessons for their students. They have to bear in mind how differentiated learning may be applied to cater to the different learning abilities of their students. While the academic issues are seemingly the most important criteria for our students, there are however, more challenging skills that they have to acquire in order to survive and thrive in their later work life. Besides conferring paper qualifications, how then can we as educators ensure that our students are prepared adequately for a challenging future? How are we as educators, able to make sure that we do not "pigeonhole people" (Lee, 2006) and put students on a track where the destination has already been predestined for them?

Our education system has opened up many avenues for our future generation. It aims to grow and develop their skills in accordance to their talents and unique interests over the decade. Every School a Good School, one of the MOE initiatives since 2011, has been the springboard for many different activities and programmes in the various schools to develop students holistically rather than focusing only on the academics. While each school is driven by its own set of visions and missions, most, if not all, the schools are converging towards the same goal, that is, to provide a positive and conducive environment for the students, allowing them to acquire the basics, but more importantly, teaching them to become confident and lifelong learners (Heng, 2011).

Read, Remember, Regurgitate

Gone are the days when all that a student had to do was to read, remember and regurgitate the facts during examinations and he or she could be reasonably sure of achieving quite a good grade. Learning this way results in not having a deep understanding of what we learn, how to make connections between the theoretical world and the real world, and how to apply the skills acquired and gain better new learning from the experience. Such a learning style hinders one's growth and development. In order to move away from this "traditional" form of learning, the syllabus is changing to allow students to develop problem-solving skills and analytical thinking. For instance, the introduction of project work has encouraged students to work in teams to come up with a presentation or product. This form of group work has no right or wrong answers nor does it provide any avenue for regurgitation. It requires creativity and the cooperation of all the team members to be able to score a good grade in the project. According to Van Velsor and Wright (2012), students lack the ability to communicate face to face and are over-dependent on technology. This form of assessment enforces a need for communication among peers and allows assessment for learning where students will gain more than what they can only read and remember from textbooks. Through these hands-on experience where they have to plan, organise, execute, present and review, they will gain a deeper understanding in the subject matter that they are learning.

Prior Knowledge, Pedagogy, Pupils' Outcomes

Today, it is indeed a challenge for the educator to be skilful in activating students' prior knowledge (including their learning style) and design a suitable pedagogy (based on students' diverse learning needs and abilities) to engage and acquire 21st century skills.

In this chapter, we will unveil some of the primary school practices in preparing our youths for the workplace.

Holistic Development: Go, Grow, Glow

In order to develop students holistically, the Ministry of Education (MOE) encourages and supports schools to develop rich learning programmes that will cater to our students' diverse talents and interests (MOE, 2010). One such school that has been motivated to evolve from the MOE initiative to provide a holistic development in students is Corporation Primary School. The introduction of the Programme for Active Learning (PAL), co-curricular activities (CCA), environmental education, student leadership and talent development promotes the development of skills beyond the textbooks so that students can **go** and experience learning outside the syllabus and classroom.

For example, the PAL lessons teach students values such as social awareness, teamwork and respect through the activities that are carried out. As part of the Primary Education Review and Implementation (PERI) recommendations accepted by MOE in 2009, PAL was introduced to strengthen the emphasis on non-academic programmes for Primary 1 and 2 students. This is in line with the key desired outcome of PERI recommendations which is to balance the acquisition of knowledge with the development of skills and values. This is to prepare our children for a more dynamic future. Conducted within curriculum time, PAL modules provide students with broad exposure in two areas — sports and outdoor education, and performing and visual arts. It aims to facilitate the well-rounded development of students in the five learning domains (cognitive, moral, social, aesthetics and physical) and help them to develop social emotional competencies (Ministry of Education, 2010). With the implementation of such programmes, students **grow** to become confident team players and independent learners. These skills allow them to build strong mental toughness in order for them to advance, aim high and **glow** in the working world.

Building the Mental Toughness to Drive the Learning: Empower, Experience, Extend

The life of our students, typically, is getting better nowadays. With the increase in socio-economic status of their parents, students are now commonly from more well-off families compared to students in the early 19th century. There is no longer a need for them to work to bring home the bread and butter for their families before heading for school. However, with the ease in getting almost anything they want, we have to admit that as educators, it is an uphill task to challenge students to work towards getting better results or strive for their best in certain tasks or competitions.

On the other hand, there is another group of students who are unable to attend school regularly because of a problematic family background. Some may end up giving up school or do badly due to lack of motivation and home support. How then is it possible for such students to be ready for the highly demanding and stressful workplace in the years to come when they do not even have the desire to get a good education? That is when we have to work on their mental toughness, and drive their desire to be able to continue learning each day. Then again, what is mental toughness?

Mental toughness is keeping strong in the face of adversity. It's the ability to keep your focus, determination and confidence despite the difficulties and pressures you encounter (Jones, Hanton, & Connaughton, 2002). It is observed that students nowadays lack a strong work ethic, focus, commitment, drive and self-motivation (Van & Wright, 2012). Most of the students whom we face in the classrooms today tend to give up easily in the face of challenges and failures. They are lacking the resilience to grit their teeth and move up from the bottom. It is then the job of the educators to bring in a positive culture in the classrooms to eliminate any negative feelings that these students may have. Reorienting psychology makes normal people stronger and more productive, as well as making high human potential actual (Seligman, 2002).

This can only happen when educators go the extra mile to talk to each and every student about their inner thoughts and emotions, be it after a test where they failed badly or a class competition which they did not manage to win. Such "pep" talks and connections with the students will allow them to have another perspective which students may not be able to see when they are indulging in their notion of failure.

Teachers should also **empower** their students to take on the responsibility to lead and hone their leadership skills. In the meantime, teachers can scaffold and guide students through the process. In the process, they will encounter and **experience** failures in the beginning but will see it as an opportunity to reflect, gain new learning and then react more positively and **extend** greater possibilities towards the matter and work towards achieving better results the next time. From this outcome, it also allows stronger teacher-student bonds being fostered as the students show no fear in sharing their innermost emotions with their teachers. This is what we educators name the "teachable moments" where we have to put aside the textbooks and handle the real issue at hand. While we impart knowledge to the students, we need to also infuse decision-making skills, long-term perspective and the ability to understand complexity to solve any problem that the students may come up with. Teachers should advise students how they should react to the problem, taking on the various perspectives of the people involved and how their actions can complicate or resolve the issue. For example, in a simple case scenario of a poor student who decides to play truant to work and earn money for the family, the student fails to consider his own future in his attempt to solve his family's problem. A vital role of the educator is to facilitate a discussion and encourage students to take the perspectives of the mother, the child and the teacher in resolving the problem. Through consideration of the different perspectives, valuable lessons are learnt to aid students in problem solving as well as building their resilience before they enter work life.

Another way of building students' mental toughness is through the promotion of reflection in their work. It is observed that students often lack reflection, self-awareness and maturity. Reflection has many facets. For example, reflecting on work enhances its meaning. Reflecting on experiences encourages insight and complex learning. We foster our own growth when we control our learning, so some reflection is best done alone. Reflection is also enhanced, however, when we ponder our learning with others (Costa & Kallick, 2008).

When educators get students to reflect, students get to act upon and process the information, synthesising and evaluating the information they have learnt from the completed assignment. Through reflection, they may be able to apply what they have learnt to contexts beyond the original situations in which the students have learnt something. Educators who promote reflective classrooms ensure that students are fully engaged in the process of making meaning. They organise instruction so that students are the producers, not just the consumers, of knowledge. To best guide students in the habits of reflection, educators will approach their role as that of "facilitator of meaning making". Students take ownership of their own learning and will be able to gain much more than just learning from their teachers. Learning thus becomes a continual process of engaging and transforming the mind (Costa & Kallick, 2008). In the event that something goes wrong, students reflect and learn from the mistakes made, which in turn allows them to garner self-awareness skills and develop maturity in their thoughts and actions.

"Once you replace negative thoughts with positive ones, you'll start having positive results" (Nelson, 2001). While we try to build students' mental toughness to prepare them for their future workplace, the positivity of the students' characters plays a major role in shaping how they think, act and reflect as well. One who always thinks of failing may not achieve as much as the one who gives it his or her all, and who shows no fear in whatever the outcome may be. Hence, setting up a positive environment allows students to grow to become more positive and this will in turn help to strengthen their mental toughness. They will be less easily defeated or give up in challenging situations that may not seem to be favourable to them. This is achieved when educators are able to encourage the students on a regular basis and feed them with positive thoughts so they can work towards greater success. Educators need to be the role model themselves and believe in this. They have to show their positivity before they can influence their students to think likewise. They can tell their students that if their thoughts are reasonable and encouraging, continue saying them to themselves. Instead of negative thoughts predicting disaster, the newer, more positive thoughts will pave the way for solutions they may have never considered before. It does take some effort on the educators' part to continue reiterating positive statements in class.

Images and sounds can also be very influential over some people's minds. If the educators know that their students respond to these, they may conjure up a particular image with its corresponding positive thoughts to give them weight — perhaps a colour that is calming to them, or an object that represents control or strength to their students. Words spoken aloud also can have a profound effect on the mind. A recent study highlighted in *Psychology Today* describes how speaking aloud helps create two forms of memory. You remember the words both from reading them and from hearing them aloud (Krull, 2010). Thus, such practices will be able to push students towards having a positive mindset which will definitely be beneficial for them in their future workplace where various other types of challenging situations await them.

Social Emotional Learning: Reflection, Relevance, Reaction

Social and emotional learning (SEL) is the acquisition of skills needed to recognise and manage emotions, develop care and concern for others, make responsible decisions, establish positive relationships and handle challenging situations effectively. Social and emotional competencies can be categorised into five domains: self-awareness, self-management, social awareness, relationship management and responsible decision making. Within each domain, there are key competencies to be exemplified.

To facilitate SEL, there are five pedagogical principles to guide the practice of teaching to achieve effective learning in pupils. They can be applied across different situations and include axioms like "go from known to unknown", "use show and tell" and "explore first, derive later". SEL can be facilitated through infusion into the formal curriculum. Teachers are the key drivers in customising their lessons to facilitate SEL through the five pedagogical principles.

1. Providing for the emotional dimension

In order for students to develop emotional skills, the learning environment has to be psychologically safe and conducive so that students feel accepted and valued. Teachers need to have the skills to provide opportunity for students to express their feelings and thoughts, and to speak without fear of being laughed at or put down. To discuss dilemmas or relevant stories, it is essential that the environment is conducive for learning, so that the students are not stressed and can express themselves and take risks in making their views heard (Ee, 2012). It is through this that they gain confidence, gather new learning and build their knowledge from the rich discussions. Students become confident in articulating their views, a skill that is vital in the workplace where effective communication is key for the sharing and exchanging of ideas to drive competitive results.

On the other hand, students from emotionally deprived home backgrounds may not be used to expressing their feelings and may even have difficulty acknowledging how they feel. Teachers need to recognise this and design their lessons using songs and poems reflecting their own feelings, so as to provide such students with non-threatening opportunities to talk about. This can be summed up as (1) touching feelings and (2) touching on feelings. A skilful teacher should be able to integrate both traits in designing a lesson such as providing a real-life scenario, e.g., one that involves a bully (suitable and authentic to the students). The teacher can elicit responses on how they feel for the characters and get the class to talk about it and how to overcome such feelings, giving examples like talking to a teacher or school counsellor for advice and help. Students can learn that anytime they encounter a problem, they are not alone and that there are other channels of help. The class can come together to create a customised song on healing the world or a customised poem on anti-bullying. This practice also provides hope and possibilities for the students when they enter the real working world and meet with setbacks or obstacles. They will then know how to deal with their feelings and become a problem solver themselves by looking for different channels for help.

2. Providing for the social dimension

In the same vein, social interaction is critical for students to develop social skills. This is necessary in order to meet the basic needs for human contact and intimacy. One fundamental relationship is that between the student and the teacher. How the student experiences this relationship directly affects the potency and credibility of the teacher, as a facilitator of SEL. Students need to experience the teacher modelling good SEL competencies when interacting with them to build rapport.

Students need to read and hear and learn from another's perspective in order for their social awareness to grow. For example, in the case of class discussion, teachers can model the idea of turn-taking where each student in the class is allowed to share their opinions or thoughts about the topic discussed. Teachers have to act as the facilitator here to encourage all students to speak up their thoughts. At the same time, they have to model active listening and feedback to the students regarding the idea shared. With this, the rest of the students will be able to learn from their teachers and therefore execute the exact skills during group work. They can provide constructive questions to their peers and the latter will also know how to react and respond to such questioning without feeling offended. On a long-term basis, students will be able to grow to become confident speakers in sharing their ideas, yet not be over-confident, and also be receptive to input and feedback. It is through this experience that learning can be reinforced with reflective questions. Teachers need to provide and structure opportunities for the acquisition and practice of social skills through peer interaction and role play. Peer interaction and perspective taking are important.

3. Reflection

As in building mental toughness, it is through reflection that pupils internalise and make personal meaning out of what they learn. Until pupils integrate social and emotional competencies into their lives, a process facilitated by reflection, these will remain theoretical and will be left behind in the classroom once the pupils step out of the door. Effective SEL teachers must provide opportunities for **reflection**, especially in terms of evaluation and application in their personal lives. Teachers can end the lesson by doing a check-out session, journal writing and conference session with the pupils. Keeping a journal for students to document any form of reflection, be it for the lessons taught or a channel for them to share any events worth mentioning that happened over the weekend is an effective way for teachers to know their students better. This form of reflection and sharing creates an amicable yet professional relationship between the teachers and students which also serves to help build students' character with a strong sense of values, ethics and social responsibility, and it assists them to manage their emotions as they advance in their growing-up years.

4. Relevance

Relevance is another key principle for facilitating SEL. Students understand and remember better when the subject matter is age-appropriate and relates to their personal experiences. Teachers can create real scenarios and provide the experiential learning so that concepts are more quickly comprehended when students see the **relevance**. For example, in English composition where students are supposed to write about a school event, students may experience anxiety at the beginning of the lesson if they have had no experience with the topic. Students who have the personal experience can share and the teacher can build on this prior experience to generate the content and introduce vocabulary to describe the event. In Mathematics, students can be brought to a supermarket to buy actual products to learn the concept of money. They will also learn empathy when they play the role of their mothers purchasing groceries for their daily needs and learn to appreciate their mothers better. It is actually a real-life enactment of working in groups when the students eventually step into working society. They not only have to recollect the knowledge learnt from their teachers and put it to use, but they also have to exhibit teamwork and active listening skills which they had learnt in schools. In a real context, students learn better and it will help them to transfer what they have learnt to other similar contexts and better prepare them for the real world.

5. Reaction

SEL involves the acquisition of skills. It is imperative that students are given the opportunity to observe the skill demonstrated and then practise it in a controlled environment with guidance before applying it in the real world. It is through the **reaction** from other students that they learn from their mistakes and get better as they progress. For example, in the role playing of different roles in a group work setting, students can take turns to be the role of a facilitator where they help to question the thoughts and ideas put forward by students. This form of knowledge-building interaction deepens their understanding of a given task and brings them together to strive for excellence. Teamwork is important to achieve organisational excellence and educators need to provide ample opportunities for students to socialise and work collaboratively.

During the CCA and values in action (VIA) projects, students experience different sets of emotions — anxiety before a competition, excitement when winning a game, devastation during a loss, frustration when team members are not cooperative, compassion and empathy when they see the less fortunate — that evoke different kinds of reactions in them. These are real scenarios and learning opportunities where the students react there and then. In certain cases where students have over-reacted, fights or quarrels may result. The teacher will then step in to mediate and resolve any misunderstanding and educate the student with the correct mindset and attitude towards the issue at hand. This aids in positive character building where students will develop an affirmative outlook in life and they will be equipped with skills in handling the future challenges they will face.

In Conclusion: Create, Connect, Contribute

Teachers are the key drivers in the learning classroom. They play a pivotal role in designing engaging lessons to ensure the successful education outcomes of their students. In a fast-changing society where demands are challenging, teachers need to hone their skills to **create** engaging lessons so that pupils are able to **connect** and make meaning from the lessons learnt and **contribute** actively and purposely to society.

References

Costa, A. L. & Kallick, B. (2008). Learning through reflection. In Costa, A. L. & Kallick, B. (eds.), *Learning and Leading with Habits of Mind*. Houston: ASCD. Chapter 12.

Ee, J. (2012). *Infusing Thinking and Social Emotional Learning in Children and Youths*. Singapore: Pearson Education Asia. Chapter 2, 14.

Heng, S. K. (2011). Message by Mr Heng Swee Keat, Minister for Education, at the Ministry of Education Work Plan Seminar on 22 September 2011 at Ngee Ann Polytechnic Convention Centre. Retrieved on 26 January 2015 from http://www.moe.gov.sg/media/speeches/2011/09/22/work-plan-sem-inar-2011.php

Jones, G., Hanton, S., & Connaughton, D. (2002). What is this thing called mental toughness? An Investigation of elite sport performers. *Journal of Applied Sport Psychology*, 14(3), 205–218.

Krull, E. (2010). *Replacing Your Negative Thoughts — Psych Central*. Retrieved on 28 January 2015 from http://psychcentral.com/lib/replacing-your-negative-thoughts/0003762

Lee, H. L. (2006). Speech by Prime Minister Lee Hsien Loong at the Teachers' Day Rally 2006 on 31 August 2006 at Singapore Expo. Retrieved on 26 January 2015 from http://www.moe.gov.sg/media/speeches/2006/sp20060831.htm

Ministry of Education (2010). *Developing Skills and Values in Pupils: Another 24 Primary Schools to Implement Programme for Active Learning from 2011*. Retrieved on 26 January 2015 from http://www.moe.gov.sg/media/ press/2010/09/developing-skills-and-values.php

Nelson, W. (2001). Retrieved on 28 January 2015 from BrainyQuote.com website: http://www.brainyquote.com/quotes/quotes/w/willienels184361.html

Seligman, M. E. P. (2002). *Handbook of Positive Psychology 2002*. Retrieved on 26 January 2015 from http://www.positiveculture.org/uploads/7/4/0/7/7407777/ seligrman_intro.pdf

Van Velsor, E. & Wright, J. (2012). *Expanding the Leadership Equation: Developing Next-Generation Leaders*. White Paper. Center for Creative Leadership. Retrieved on 7 February 2015 from http://www.ccl.org/Leadership/pdf/research/Expanding LeadershipEquation.pdf

Chapter 19

Self-Regulation of AD(H)D Habits

Chelsea Chew

AD(H)D: Prevalence and Characteristics

Amongst children and teenagers all over the world, around 5–7% have attention-deficit (hyperactivity) disorder (AD(H)D) (Willcutt, 2012). A study involving young adults found that 10% of them have what is termed subclinical AD(H)D (Gudjonsson *et al.*, 2009), whereby the individuals have features of AD(H)D that do not meet the full criteria for a diagnosis of AD(H)D. The presence of AD(H)D can be identified by the presentation of certain traits using the *Diagnostic and Statistical Manual of Mental Disorders, Fifth Edition* (DSM-V) (American Psychiatric Association, 2013). According to the DSM-V, there are three subtypes of AD(H)D:

1. Predominantly inattentive subtype
2. Predominantly hyperactive-impulsive subtype
3. Combined type

The criteria for a diagnosis of AD(H)D, as listed in the DSM-V, are reproduced here:

1. **Predominantly inattentive subtype:** six or more symptoms of inattention for children up to age 16, or five or more for adolescents 17 and older and adults; symptoms of inattention have been present

for at least six months, and they are inappropriate for the person's developmental level:

- Often fails to give close attention to details or makes careless mistakes in schoolwork, at work, or with other activities
- Often has trouble holding attention on tasks or play activities
- Often does not seem to listen when spoken to directly
- Often does not follow through on instructions and fails to finish schoolwork, chores or duties in the workplace (e.g., loses focus, easily side-tracked)
- Often has trouble organising tasks and activities
- Often avoids, dislikes, or is reluctant to do tasks that require mental effort over a long period of time (such as schoolwork or homework)
- Often loses things necessary for tasks and activities (e.g., school materials, pencils, books, tools, wallets, keys, paperwork, eyeglasses, mobile telephones)
- Often easily distracted
- Often forgetful in daily activities

2. **Predominantly hyperactive-impulsive subtype:** six or more symptoms of hyperactivity-impulsivity for children up to age 16, or five or more for adolescents 17 and older and adults; symptoms of hyperactivity-impulsivity have been present for at least six months to an extent that is disruptive and inappropriate for the person's developmental level:

- Often fidgets with or taps hands or feet, or squirms in seat
- Often leaves seat in situations when remaining seated is expected
- Often runs about or climbs in situations where it is not appropriate (adolescents or adults may be limited to feeling restless)
- Often unable to play or take part in leisure activities quietly
- Often "on the go", acting as if "driven by a motor"
- Often talks excessively
- Often blurts out an answer before a question has been completed
- Often has trouble waiting his or her turn
- Often interrupts or intrudes on others (e.g., butts into conversations or games)

3. Individuals with the combined subtype of AD(H)D meet the criteria for both categories of symptoms: inattention plus hyperactive-impulsive subtypes.

People with AD(H)D show a persistent pattern of either inattention or hyperactivity or both that hinders their functioning. Individuals with subclinical AD(H)D have less than the requisite number of symptoms for their age. Students who have academic difficulties may report having a combination of the abovementioned symptoms to various degrees of severity. While their teachers or their families may regard this as an excuse, the condition is a legitimate one — AD(H)D has distinct neurological markers such as reductions in the size of the frontal lobes (Wolosin *et al.*, 2009).

AD(H)D: Impact on Grades and Workplace Performance

AD(H)D has a definite negative impact on grades, resulting in many students with AD(H)D being streamed into less academically challenging courses. It was found that students with AD(H)D have lower college grade point averages (GPA) and have higher dropout and academic probation rates than their peers without AD(H)D (Heiligenstein *et al.*, 1998). In fact, attention problems were found to be the strongest negative predictor of college GPA (Schwanz, Palm, & Brallier, 2007). Adults with AD(H)D also reported having more academic difficulties such as taking longer to complete assignments and having to go through material repeatedly to understand it than adults without AD(H)D do (Lewandowski *et al.*, 2008).

Initially, AD(H)D was believed to diminish after puberty. However, there is mounting evidence that affected individuals do not outgrow the disorder by adulthood. Issues of hyperactivity abate but difficulties with inattention and distractibility persist. In adulthood, a more challenging set of AD(H)D symptoms gains prominence — those symptoms related to executive function. Executive function includes the ability to plan, prioritise and organise, in most cases, to achieve a certain long-term aim. All through primary school, and much of secondary school, students are provided with external structure, e.g., short-term assignments or projects with firm deadlines with the requisite punishments as deterrents if the deadlines are not met. As individuals advance to adulthood, they are required to take on more responsibilities, encounter less structure, and have to use their executive functions to plan in advance, set priorities and stay organised as they manage themselves and their resources of time and money. In a study on the workplace performance of AD(H)D workers, supervisors of AD(H)D workers who were blind to the diagnoses of the AD(H)D group found them to be more impaired in performing assigned tasks, in punctuality, and in general, managing time properly compared to non-AD(H)D workers (Murphy & Barkley, 2007).

AD(H)D Strengths and the Workplace

In addition to various challenges, AD(H)D individuals present with a multitude of strengths. Due to their high levels of energy, they are often exuberant and enthusiastic, which would help them to promote a cause or sell an idea or a product. AD(H)D individuals are also highly creative and can come up with a multitude of ideas quickly. This could see them choosing careers in the creative fields such as advertising, public relations and design. A number of people with AD(H)D are also adventurous, which permits them to take risks such as in business. A combination of creative thinking and adventurousness could result in an AD(H)D businessman thinking out of the box, changing the way things are traditionally done and risking setbacks while doing so. Further, people with AD(H)D are highly comfortable with chaos and disorder as they often have to deal with chaos such as crises due to procrastination and poor planning. They are energised by chaos and emergency situations, and deal with them much better than non-AD(H)D individuals, who may be crippled into inaction. This trait could see AD(H)D individuals working in emergency wards, in crisis teams, and as police personnel or firemen.

A vital characteristic of AD(H)D necessities mention. In much the same way that AD(H)D results in low levels of attention when the individual is bored, it results in hyperfocus, or the ability to focus intensely for long periods of time, when the individual is highly interested in something. It is this trait of AD(H)D that allows AD(H)D individuals to become experts in their fields of interest: once they hone in on something that is highly stimulating for them, they can devote much time and energy to mastering it.

There are numerous successful individuals diagnosed with AD(H)D. The more famous ones amongst them include Robin Williams, who was highly exuberant as a person and very successful as an actor, having won a number of acting awards for his different performances. Another is Michael Phelps, the most decorated Olympian of all time, who garnered an astounding 22 Olympic medals. As he was growing up, his mother, an educator, refused to allow Michael to be limited by his AD(H)D. Instead, she leveraged on his AD(H)D strengths of hyperactivity, or the need to be physically active, on swimming (Dutton, 2007). Sir Richard Branson, the founder of the Virgin Group (which includes Virgin Airlines), uses his creativity to generate a multitude of new ideas and innovations in his businesses and relies on his sense of adventure to daringly experiment with them, such as his ventures into space travel.

Transiting to the Workplace: AD(H)D and Self-Regulation

Transiting to the workplace upon leaving school is an important step for youths. As illustrated, having AD(H)D bestows the individual with specific traits that can help the individual's career or hinder it. How then, do individuals with AD(H)D ensure that they are able to leverage on their AD(H)D strengths whilst minimising their AD(H)D weaknesses when these weaknesses, at times, threaten to outweigh their talents and skills?

AD(H)D has been touted as essentially a disorder of self-regulation (Barkley, 2012), whereby people with AD(H)D lack the ability to spontaneously set goals, monitor their use of various strategies, self-evaluate the outcomes, and refine the process continuously to achieve their goals. From this point of view, then, training AD(H)D youths to be more self-regulated would be tantamount to targeting what can be deemed their core deficit. Importantly, self-regulation has been found to have a strong relationship with job success; it outweighs talent in job success (Abele & Wiese, 2008).

Zimmerman (2002) defines self-regulation as the processes we use to activate and sustain our thoughts, behaviors and emotions in order to reach our goals. Self-regulation comprises a whole host of strategies such as goal setting, time management, seeking social assistance, self-evaluation, and self-consequences. Self-regulation can be applied to a variety of contexts in which the individual has to be responsible for and autonomous in his behaviour. It is this applicability of self-regulation strategies that makes it suitable as a basket of techniques for helping AD(H)D youths transit to the workplace.

Transiting to the Workplace: Self-Regulation Techniques for AD(H)D Youths

A standard series of steps are essential in self-regulation: the individual (1) first sets a specific goal, (2) monitors his or her present use of strategies, (3) evaluates the outcomes with these strategies, and (4) adapts as necessary the use of these strategies to enhance his or her performance.

Regarding the first step, goal setting, people with AD(H)D do not automatically set goals, especially when they have to manage goals along a timeline, and this impacts their ability to get things done. In the second step, monitoring the use of strategies, individuals with AD(H)D would have to be highly cognisant of, and vigilant to, what they are currently doing to produce certain outcomes. This would mean being very alert to the specific strategies, even self-defeating ones, such as negative self-talk. Daily recording would help to foster accurate self-monitoring. In the third step, the AD(H)D individuals would judge if the strategies utilised have helped them to achieve their goals, or if they are deemed less than satisfactory. Finally, in the last step, they would have to refine the strategies used or try different strategies.

1. **Goal setting.** People with AD(H)D would do well to plan their long-term career goals. In long-term planning for their careers, to ensure career success, AD(H)D individuals need to choose careers that magnify or at least leverage on their strengths whilst downplaying their weaknesses. A distinction needs to be made between careers and jobs. Careers are jobs in a particular field with a certain nature of work; specific jobs come with particular companies, and supervisors with different styles.

For AD(H)D individuals to come to a decision about their long-term career goals, an understanding of their strengths with simultaneous acknowledgement of the different AD(H)D weaknesses they have would be vital. For instance, certain AD(H)D individuals may be motivated by monetary rewards and will work hard if thus motivated. In this case, choosing a commission-based career will prove highly rewarding. If some AD(H)D individuals are unsure about committing to a particular career, instead of drifting from job to job without a long-term goal, it cannot be emphasised enough that they should approach a career counsellor and take a career inventory or assessment of interests to receive some guidance on what they are suitable for.

Goal setting is all the more vital because it is not something that comes naturally to people with AD(H)D. A "rule of five" with each of the five fingers of one hand representing a goal works to help people with AD(H)D keep their goals in the forefront of their minds. The thumb could stand for the long-term goal, or "where and in what position I see myself working in fives years". The first finger would represent a shorter term goal of "where I would be in a year". The second finger would represent work goals to be achieved within the next month and the third finger, goals to be achieved at work within the day. Finally, the last finger would represent goals to be achieved at work within the next half-hour. While it seems unnecessary to break goals down into steps of one month and minute steps of half-hours, it is very much needed for AD(H)D individuals, who have difficulties planning and whose minds tend to wander. If there is no pressing deadline to get something done quickly, it is very easy for the AD(H)D mind to wander off at tangents, to other more interesting and otherwise "pressing" concerns. For some AD(H)D individuals, even goals of half-hour blocks could prove too long to stay focused on. In this case, smaller blocks of 15 minutes or less could be more appropriate.

2. **Emotional regulation.** Once the goals have been set, whatever they are, the AD(H)D individuals' emotions would have to be regulated to gear them towards those goals. A number of AD(H)D individuals have low self-esteem and high levels of self-doubt due to their repeated failures or

inability to perform up to their levels of potential. Their battered sense of self and low self-efficacy prevents them from approaching and seizing opportunities and results in a perpetual cycle of low self-worth and missed opportunities for performance. In the workplace, these feelings would seriously hinder their ability to meet their career goals, be they long-term or short-term goals.

To tackle these feelings, self-regulation of one's feelings is vital here. People with AD(H)D need to monitor their feelings regularly, and be highly alert to when they are bogged down by low self-esteem, self-doubt, and consequently, avoidance.

- Low self-esteem is characterised by thoughts whereby one puts oneself down, such as, "I dislike myself", and "I am a lousy person". These thoughts are most likely to occur after yet another failed attempt at reaching a particular goal, which activates memories of many other "failures" in the AD(H)D individual's mind.

  Such thoughts only serve to make one feel shame and render one emotionally weak to engage in the process of self-regulation, whereby one has to monitor the outcomes and refine the strategies used. In the worst case scenario, it could cause the individual with AD(H)D to spiral downwards into depression. The AD(H)D person has to say instead, "I love and accept myself for who I am, warts and all" and "I will slip up every now and then, but it is okay, it is not a sign of failure but feedback as part of the self-regulation process".

- Self-doubt or low self-efficacy manifests as feelings of inability such as "I can't achieve, I have AD(H)D", or "how can I do it, it's too hard for me, I've failed many times before". These feelings are likely to become self-fulfilling prophecies. Once again, individuals with AD(H)D have to attempt to quell these thoughts with opposing thoughts such as "If other people with AD(H)D can achieve, so can I, thinking positively is one step!" or "I believe that I can, and I will".

- Avoidance is often an offshoot and a natural progression of having associated feelings of failure, and low self-efficacy with certain tasks. To break the cycle of feelings of dread, and low self-efficacy and avoidance,

avoidance in its different forms, such as delaying or refusing work, would have to be replaced by approach strategies which could be very short encounters with the work that is being avoided. As the AD(H)D individuals attempt to approach tasks that they typically avoid, thoughts such as "it is something that I can accomplish" or "I will start with a small bit. See, it wasn't that dreadful at all, why am I avoiding it? I would have to be engaged in."

Due to difficulties with executive function, an adult with AD(H)D finds it highly challenging to manage time. This causes difficulties determining how long tasks take. Hence, how much time to allot for each task, and the problem manifests as punctuality issues and difficulties completing tasks. As reported by Murphy and Barkley (2007), these are the key complaints of supervisors of AD(H)D workers.

3. **Regulation of time to ensure punctuality.** Most individuals with AD(H)D have no concept of "buffer time" or allowances of time. If they are expected to start work at 9 a.m., they would frequently assume the "best case scenario" of not having to wait for public transport and ideal traffic conditions even during peak-hour traffic. Due to the impairments in their executive function, many adults take years or decades to learn from mistakes in late-coming. Each time the AD(H)D adult is late, he or she typically repeats the same mistakes, resulting in the same outcomes.

Self-regulation has to be employed here. Once they become aware of the repeated negative outcomes, individuals with AD(H)D have to monitor their use of time while getting ready for work and change their strategies so as to be punctual. Alternative strategies to use so as to be punctual include, firstly, the aim to arrive 15 minutes earlier than stipulated. Secondly, buffer time for various traffic conditions, using the prevailing traffic conditions, such as peak-hour traffic, as an estimate, would have to be factored in.

Even with these two strategies, AD(H)D individuals will still be late due once again to their easy distractibility. To elaborate, while preparing to get ready for work, they could be seized by the desire to find out about the latest movie they heard about. As they delve into the net, they would chance upon other distractions. Frequent self-monitoring of the use of strategies (whether deliberate or accidental, and resulting in either positive or negative outcomes) in attempting to go to work punctually would allow them to glean important information on what could be changed to achieve better punctuality outcomes.

Finally, time habits, like other habits, may not be changed overnight. Lest any failure in being punctual results in feelings of low-self-esteem and self-efficacy, allowances must be afforded to oneself with the reminder that another incidence of lateness is yet another piece of feedback to oneself on what would need to be changed in the self-regulation process towards punctuality.

4. **Regulation of time to ensure productivity.** The other main complaint of supervisors of AD(H)D workers besides punctuality is their inability to hand in work in a timely manner. In much the same manner as being punctual for work, workers with AD(H)D would have to evaluate whether the strategies they have used previously for being punctual worked, and if not, to devise new strategies for improving productivity outcomes. When estimating the amount of time needed to get a particular task done, workers with AD(H)D tend to be grossly off the mark and often imagine that a task can be completed within a significantly shorter period of time than it would really take.

In one strategy to help AD(H)D individuals better estimate how long a task would take and plan ahead, once again, "best case scenarios" would have to be replaced with scenarios involving buffer time for all sorts of contingencies. Another strategy would be the use of short-term and time-limited goals as the AD(H)D mind does not know how to work with long periods of time and will lose focus. Thus, when workers with AD(H)D have to complete a particular task, they could work in "sprints" of around 15 minutes with specific small goals to be accomplished rather than over a longer period of time, e.g., an hour.

Further suggestions for increasing productivity would include any sort of structure, or anything that fosters organisation. As the AD(H)D mind does not naturally organise information, physical organisers in the form of diaries, schedules and timetables would help immensely the AD(H)D worker to remember tasks, and allocate and plan tasks along a timeline. As another reason for low productivity is disorganisation and subsequent loss of needed materials, structure in the form of coloured folders, multiple electronic folders and subfolders, shelves and drawers would have to be utilised. The self-regulation of the use of the different strategies would provide important information on what works best for each individual with AD(H)D.

5. **Seeking help to ensure productivity.** Finally, as becoming good time managers so as to ensure productivity and the timely submission of tasks can be a lengthy process for AD(H)D individuals, workers with AD(H)D should utilise help-seeking, yet another self-regulatory process. This could include the request for aids in the form of role models for time management, which would allow the workers with AD(H)D to identify the ways in which they manage time differently when setting priorities, planning and carrying out activities.

Environments where the AD(H)D workers do not have to set up their own structure would be ideal for them. Accountability to a higher authority is a form of external structure that would provide tremendous help in promoting task completion, especially when planning over a long period of time is needed. Hence, workers with AD(H)D could put in specific requests for someone to report to, resulting in close supervision with firm and short-term deadlines set by the supervisors in long-drawn projects.

Lest individuals with AD(H)D feel disheartened about the challenges they face in preparation for the workplace, a recap of the many strengths that workers with AD(H)D bring to the workplace is in order, such as exuberance, creativity, an ability to take risks and an ability to handle chaos. With the consistent use of self-regulatory strategies which in essence, is about changing the strategies — deliberate or otherwise — that one is using to achieve certain goals, AD(H)D workers would be well poised to minimise their weaknesses and fully leverage on their strengths to achieve success in their chosen careers.

References

Abele, A. E. & Wiese, B. S. (2008). The nomological network of self-management strategies and career success. *Journal of Occupational and Organizational Psychology*, 81, 733–749.

American Psychiatric Association (2013). *Diagnostic and Statistical Manual of Mental Disorders (5th ed.)*. Washington, DC: Author.

Barkley, R. A. (2012). *Executive Functioning and Self-Regulation: Extended Phenotype, Synthesis, and Clinical Implications*. New York: Guilford Publications.

Dutton, J. (2007, April/May). *ADHD Parenting Advice from Michael Phelps' Mom*. Retrieved on 15 February 2015 from http://www.additudemag.com/AD(H)D/article/1998.html

Gudjonsson, G. H., Sigurdsson, J. F., Eyjolfsdottir, G. A., Smari, J., & Young, S. (2009). The relationship between satisfaction with life, AD(H)D symptoms, and associated problems among university students. *Journal of Attention Disorders*, 12(6), 507–515.

Heiligenstein, E., Conyers, L. M., Berns, A. R., & Millar, M. A. (1998). Preliminary normative data on DSM-IV Attention Deficit Hyperactivity Disorder in college students. *Journal of American College Health*, 46, 185–188.

Lewandowski, L. J., Lovett, B. J., Codding, R. S., & Godron, M. (2008). Symptoms of AD(H)D and academic concerns in college students with and without AD(H)D diagnoses. *Journal of Attention Disorders*, 12, 156–161.

Murphy, K. R. & Barkley, R. A. (2007). Occupation functioning in adults with AD(H)D. *The AD(H)D Report*, 15(1), 6–10.

Schwanz, K. A., Palm, L. J., & Brallier, S. A. (2007). Attention problem and hyperactivity as predictors of college grade point average. *Journal of Attention Disorders*, 11, 368–373.

Willcutt, E. G. (2012). The prevalence of DSM-IV attention-deficit/hyperactivity disorder: A meta-analytic review. *Neurotherapeutics*, 9(3), 490–499.

Wolosin, S. M., Richardson, M. E., Hennessey, J. G., Denckla, M. B., & Mostofsky, S. H. (2009). Abnormal cerebral cortex structure in children with AD(H)D. *Human Brain Mapping*, 30(1), 175–184.

Zimmerman, B. J. (2002). Becoming a self-regulated learner: An overview. *Theory into Practice*, 41(2), 64–70.

Chapter 20

Using Positive Psychology to Help Young Adults with High Functioning Autism Transit to the Workplace

Chelsea Chew

There are purportedly 50,000 individuals with autism spectrum disorders (ASD) in Singapore (Autism Resource Centre, n.d.) of which some are in our mainstream schools. Those who manage to stay in the mainstream school system have normal cognitive abilities, which is usually pegged at IQs of over 80 (Gabig, 2011). In a given population, around a quarter to a third of individuals with ASD will be high-functioning (Ozonoff, Dawson, & McPartland, 2002), and be able to demonstrate relatively normal learning and language skills. Given that fact and the estimate that many more individuals with high-functioning autism (HFA) will be diagnosed in the future (Centre for Disease Control, 2014), this means that a substantial number of youths with HFA are, and more will be, in our mainstream school system.

Characteristics of ASD

Individuals with HFA have a cluster of symptoms that might occur in any combination that fall into the mild range. According to the fifth edition of the *Diagnostic and Statistical Manual of Mental Disorders* (DSM-V), ASD is characterised by the following (excerpted from the DSM-V, American Psychiatric Association, 2013):

A. Persistent deficits in social communication and social interaction across multiple contexts, as manifested by the following, currently or by history:

   1. Deficits in social-emotional reciprocity, ranging, for example, from abnormal social approach and failure of normal back-and-forth conversation to reduced sharing of emotions or affect.
   2. Deficits in nonverbal communicative behaviors used for social interaction, for example, from abnormalities in eye contact and body language to deficits in understanding gestures.
   3. Deficits in developing, maintaining, and understanding relationships, ranging, for example, from difficulties adjusting behavior to suit various social contexts to difficulties in making friends.

B. Restricted, repetitive patterns of behavior, interests, or activities, as manifested by at least two of the following, currently or by history:

   1. Stereotyped or repetitive motor movements, use of objects, or speech (e.g., simple motor stereotypies, idiosyncratic phrases).
   2. Insistence on sameness, inflexible adherence to routines, or ritualised patterns of verbal/nonverbal behavior (e.g., extreme distress at small changes, difficulties with transitions, rigid thinking patterns).
   3. Highly restricted, fixated interests that are abnormal in intensity or focus (e.g, excessively circumscribed or perseverative interest).
   4. Hyper- or hyporeactivity to sensory input or unusual interests in sensory aspects of the environment (e.g., apparent indifference to pain/temperature, adverse response to specific sounds or textures, visual fascination with lights or movement).

The examples given for each characteristic are merely illustrative, and not exhaustive; suffice it to say that each characteristic should be viewed as a guiding concept. Taking the last characteristic listed, persons with HFA can present with any type of sensory peculiarity, ranging from hearing, to senses of sight, smell, taste and touch. Individuals with autism who were diagnosed before the publication of DSM-V were given the label of Asperger syndrome if they had higher than average IQs and developed speech and language abilities earlier than expected, as the DSM-IV-TR (American Psychiatric Association, 2000) included Asperger's disorder. Individuals with Asperger syndrome are also classified as high-functioning.

Obstacles to Successful Employment

In Singapore, Roland Tay started a café called Professor Brawn Café (Kok, 2014) which primarily hires workers who have ASD. He pays his workers market rates for their services, and it is this type of employment — competitive employment, where individuals with HFA may have to compete with others for the same work for the same salary — that potential workers with HFA are encouraged to aim for. Nevertheless, there are several challenges to overcome if workers with HFA are to be successfully employed through competitive employment.

As the characteristics of ASD are less obvious and are of a lower intensity in people with HFA, they may not be easily discerned by the casual observer, or even school teachers. However, the challenges are certainly present, and people with HFA straddle between autism and living within the wider community. Upon graduation from school, they face the challenge of navigating the workplace. Due to each individual's unique set of challenges within the spectrum, without intervention, even though they have much to contribute, they are likely to struggle with firstly, obtaining, and then keeping, a job (Taylor & Seltzer, 2011).

Social: The major obstacle to successful employment cited by employers relates to the social realm (Hillier *et al.*, 2007). Workers with HFA struggle to communicate with their co-workers and supervisors due to their difficulties with firstly recognising the existence of social rules and understanding social boundaries, and taking social perspectives (including the impact of their behaviour on others' opinions of them), and then reading others' facial expressions and tone of voice in their social interactions (Muller *et al.*, 2003).

These result in a host of issues in their workplace: doing their colleagues' work without getting due recognition, being unfairly blamed for their co-workers' mistakes, being deliberately taken advantage of in terms of work duties, and being bullied outright through social exclusion and teasing (Camarena & Sarigiani, 2009). In fact, even when they were not bullied, an inability to integrate with their co-workers through perhaps their inability to foster friendships was seen by their employers as a major obstacle to employment success (Hillier *et al.*, 2007).

Comorbid disorders: Another issue highly pertinent to ASD and HFA is the level of comorbidities with other disorders. A large percentage of individuals with ASD, and by extension, HFA, have comorbid psychiatric diagnoses of various anxiety disorders such as specific phobias, obsessive-compulsive disorder and depression. A significantly large proportion of them also have AD(H)D (Taylor & Seltzer, 2011). With AD(H)D deficits, executive functions such as planning, prioritising, and time management are affected, leading many supervisors to comment that individuals with HFA are unable to work independently without set goals (Hiller *et al.*, 2007).

Even if they do not have comorbid diagnoses, most individuals with HFA would demonstrate at least one of the psychiatric disorders commonly experienced by this population at a subclinical level. For instance, a worker with HFA might fixate on negative experiences, and keep replaying them in his mind. Another worker who works as a server may engage in obsessive behaviours when cleaning the customers' tables such as cleaning every corner carefully. Sensorial issues such as hypersensitivity to, for example, sounds as innocuous as the humming of the air-conditioner could add to their distress. Their difficulties navigating the social realm, trying to fit in, sensorial issues and fear of the unknown in their workplaces result in a high level of stress and anxiety (Hendricks, 2010) which interferes with their work performance.

Strengths in Individuals with HFA

In attempts to get persons with ASD to fit in with the rest of society, ways in which they are deficiently different are highlighted as the foci for remediation. However, individuals with ASD, and also HFA, are wired differently from the average individual and due attention has to be given to their strengths, as much as to their weaknesses, if they are to fulfil their potential. According to Temple Grandin, a successful professor in animal science who is well-known for having ASD, individuals with HFA have many strengths that can be leveraged on in the workplace (Gradin, 2014).

Special interest areas: One highly notable strength of individuals with HFA is their special interest areas. From a very young age, individuals with HFA demonstrate what are commonly termed obsessions. They would spend an inordinate amount of time on topics or activities that interest them greatly, be they particular insects, dinosaurs, modes of transportation, or drawing spacecraft and constructing with Lego bricks. As a result, they develop specialised skills in their respective areas of interest that make them experts in what they spend most of their time doing (Winter-Messiers, 2007).

For too long, persons with HFA have been told to drop their obsessive interests so as to appear normal; however, these interests could be leveraged on in the workplace. In fact, employers report appreciating the high levels of technical skills and the single-minded focus on their interests amongst individuals with HFA in their areas of expertise (Muller *et al.*, 2003). It is precisely their obsessions that give workers with HFA an edge over others. A number of HFA individuals have more than one obsession, or have past obsessions for which they have accumulated a wealth of knowledge and skill, thus increasing the number of special interest areas which could be tapped on in employment.

Visual processing ability: As reported by Grandin (2014), people with ASD think in pictures rather than in words. Due to this ability, Grandin can imagine and visualise entire processes as if she is watching a movie while she is designing livestock facilities. Information is stored in her mind like in a CD-ROM, and when a certain memory is needed, she can access it by playing it like a video. Few other people with ASD have made their strengths in visual processing known in as articulate and widespread a manner as Grandin, but it has been observed consistently that individuals with autism across the spectrum are able to process information much better when pictures are given instead of words.

Related to the superior visual learning style are acute attention to visual details and having a well-developed visual memory. Indeed, it has been noted that many individuals with HFA are able to design and draw highly intricate and sophisticated drawings from a very young age. Employers have also reported valuing the ability of HFA individuals to pay attention to details that others miss (Muller *et al.*, 2003). The potential for tapping into this strength is huge — visual processing is needed in careers ranging from design (of art pieces, buildings, equipment) to mechanics (of vehicles, computers, appliances).

Besides these two strengths, there are other strengths that can be the flip side of the deficits of ASD. Generally, highly prized strengths of workers with ASD include their hard working nature, their focus on their jobs, and their trustworthiness as seen by their low rates of absenteeism. Other strengths of workers with ASD include their ability to take on jobs that are unattractive to other workers due to the repetitive or socially isolative nature of the jobs (Stankova & Trajkovski, 2010). Although individuals with ASD have obsessive interests and usually a technical area of expertise, a wide range of careers appeal to them, even those that involve social interactions such as sales, and hospitality (Muller *et al.*, 2003).

Positive Psychology

In the field of ASD, the key theoretical orientation has been behaviourism, whereby individuals with ASD are trained through reinforcement to alter their maladaptive behaviours and learn new ones. While that is certainly a useful approach for ASD individuals as we mould them to fit into our society, it has to be paired with a philosophy which focuses on enhancing human strengths rather than addressing behavioural issues, especially given that the strengths of individuals with ASD have been overlooked. Positive psychology, which focuses on positive experiences, positive relationships, positive institutions and positive psychological states (Seligman & Csikszentmihalyi, 2000), is well poised to provide the missing link.

Essentially, positive psychology is focused on enhancing happiness and well-being instead of treating diseases or problems. Positive psychology is concerned with the strengths that allow people and institutions to flourish. Key topics within positive psychology are happiness, optimism, mindfulness, flow, character strengths and virtues, hope, positive thinking and resilience. The premise underpinning positive psychology is that people do want to have meaningful and fulfilling lives and to bring forth the best in themselves so as to enhance their experiences at work and at play. When people are at their best, they achieve happiness (Seligman, 2009).

While positive psychology has been applied to the workplace, it has not been discussed in relation to individuals with ASD in the workplace. Specific aspects of positive psychology especially pertinent to individuals with HFA functioning in competitive employment with some supports are elucidated here, with the acronym SUFE, which stands for strengths, unity, forgiveness and enthusiasm. These four positive experiences and states expounded upon here were chosen as they target key aspects of HFA and can be operationalised in as concrete a manner as possibilities to facilitate application.

1. **Strengths — use strengths, outsource flaws:** Amongst the supports for job placement most impactful for successful employment is career matching whereby individuals with HFA are matched not just on educational qualifications, interests and skills to potential careers, but also on personality traits, social skills and comorbidities. In the identification of potential careers, what is crucial is whether individuals with HFA can leverage on their strengths to the hilt with few innate work habits needing development.

   Once the specific career with a presumed set of work duties is identified, the next step is to look for a particular job whereby the key duties play up the strengths of individuals with HFA; the supervisors are supportive; and the work surroundings are suitable. It is advised that during the job application stage, applicants with HFA state very explicitly their specific set of strengths and flaws and the expectation that for success, most of their time would be devoted to duties leveraging on their strengths. Information regarding HFA is also to be provided to enlighten the human resource personnel.

Further, at this stage and subsequently, requests for supervisors who are committed to picking out the strengths of individuals with HFA and/or are willing to modify tasks to enhance these strengths on a long-term basis would be made. Ideally, tasks could be structured such that a large proportion of the HFA individual's time at work would be spent using his or her strengths so as to improve the productivity of the organisation while enhancing his or her overall well-being.

To allow individuals with HFA to further leverage on their strengths, job tasks may have to be modified from their original forms. In general, tasks appropriate for individuals with HFA would be explicitly defined in terms of how they are to be performed and would be predictable. Visual schedules, checklists, and clear visual instructions which capitalise on abilities in visual processing could be given to enhance chances for success and to consequently permit the individuals with HFA to demonstrate their strengths at the workplace.

Finally, in modifying the tasks to permit success, it is important that the supervisors allow adequate time for learning so as to reduce anxiety on the part of individuals with HFA. In terms of the physical work environment, to minimise discomfort, workplace modifications include the reduction or elimination of sensorial stimulation deemed overwhelming for the particular individual with HFA, such as smells or lights. Crucially, the tasks that individuals with HFA find particularly hard, such as those that involve social negotiations that are unpredictable or otherwise provoke anxiety, are to be passed to colleagues whose strengths lie in their ability to handle them.

2. **Unity — unity at all levels:** It has been noted that individuals with HFA have difficulties integrating socially and encounter a number of social difficulties in the workplace, such as being bullied or not receiving due recognition for their work. To ward off such problems, positive psychology demonstrated in positive institutions would have to be practised; in this case, the positive characteristic of unity at the level of the organisation, between different levels of the organisation, and between co-workers. The ethos of unity would have to be a defining characteristic of the institution whereby the workers with HFA know

that there will be long-term support and they can ask for help from different levels of the organisation.

Between supervisors and supervisees, there should be an understanding that the supervisors would want to retain the workers with HFA, and be willing to help them succeed. The supervisors should be approachable and be amongst the first people to approach if the workers with HFA encounter difficulties, before the problems snowball into major crises. The positive psychological state of unity within an institution also applies to links between co-workers. It extends to colleagues helping the workers with HFA navigate any complexities such as understanding job demands, workplace rules, and workplace polices.

Finally, and critically, unity at the workplace would mean that workers with HFA are not excluded due to their awkwardness in making friends, but intentionally included in social activities. Through these friendships, colleagues of workers with HFA can help to facilitate understanding of workplace social situations and share communication strategies to be used with external parties or other colleagues. Social integration and support would go a long way towards warding off bullying, unhappiness and depression at the workplace (Wilczynski, Trammell, & Clarke, 2013).

3. **Forgiveness — quick forgiveness of self and others:** Individuals with HFA typically experience high levels of anxiety, as evidenced by the high level of comorbid anxiety disorders. Frequently, workers with HFA worry about the unknown because they are concerned that they would not know what to do and would make mistakes. When they make mistakes due to their characteristic flaws, they can be fixated on them and be worried about the next mistake, and this fuels their anxiety, reducing their effectiveness at work. To counter this, in addition to seeking help from their co-workers within a climate of unity, workers with HFA need to cultivate the positive emotion of forgiveness.

When they make mistakes, they should say to themselves that "I forgive myself" for the errors made, and "I have many strengths though like everyone else, I would slip up every now and then". This would have to be executed the moment they utter something disparaging about their performance or themselves. Workers with HFA may have to be alerted to their own put-downs by their supervisors or their co-workers. A general strategy for co-workers of HFA individuals would be to ask what is going on when they notice the workers with HFA looking out of sorts and to coach them into forgiveness and quickly letting go of the upsetting event to prevent the workers with HFA from obsessing about it.

In the same way that workers with HFA get upset with themselves for sometimes minor mistakes, they can get disappointed and distrustful of others for various transgressions. Within a climate of unity in the workplace, it is psychologically healthier for the workers with HFA to simply forgive than to be wary of their colleagues. Once again, the importance of quickly letting go of upsets, in this case with others, has to be underscored. Besides workers with HFA, supervisors of HFA and other workers in the organisation have to learn to quickly let go of upsets with individuals with HFA for characteristic oversights.

4. **Enthusiasm — enthusiasm for the job:** As discussed, individuals with HFA have many comorbid disorders or issues such as anxiety, obsessiveness and depression. These are all negative emotions. Instead of taking the typical approach of directly minimising them, the philosophy of positive psychology can be applied here once again. Enthusiasm, being an opposite positive emotion, can act as a panacea for the host of negative feelings workers with HFA may experience at the workplace. By increasing feelings of enthusiasm, negative feelings naturally would not be able to take centre stage.

Workers with HFA could start the day with the declaration "I'm enthusiastic about what I do" or "I'm enthusiastic working here with my boss/with my colleagues". Pronouncements of this manner will go a long way towards immunising the workers with HFA from negative emotions throughout the day. In fact, this action could even be carried out by other workers in the organisation, to increase their positive feelings in the workplace.

To summarise, positive psychology, through the use of a strengths-based approach in the choice and creation of the specific duties for workers with

HFA, by instituting unity at all levels in the organisation, by fostering forgiveness on the part of the workers with HFA, and by generating enthusiasm for the specific job, can have a definite positive impact on the employment status of workers with HFA. The ability to have a meaningful life with happiness through job fulfilment is certainly within the reach of workers with HFA with the application of positive psychology techniques.

References

American Psychiatric Association (2000). *Diagnostic and Statistical Manual of Mental Disorders (4th ed., text revision)*. Washington, DC: Author.

American Psychiatric Association (2013). *Diagnostic and Statistical Manual of Mental Disorders (5th ed.)*. Washington, DC: Author.

Autism Resource Centre (n.d.). Frequently Asked Questions — On Autism. Retrieved from http://www.autism.org.sg/main/faq.php?cat=autism

Camarena, P. M., & Sarigiani, P.A. (2009). Postsecondary educational aspirations of high-functioning adolescents with autism spectrum disorders and their parents. *Focus on Autism and Other Developmental Disabilities*, 24(2), 115–128.

Centre for Disease Control (2014). *CDC Estimates 1 in 68 Children Has Been Identified with Autism Spectrum Disorder*. Retrieved from http://www.cdc.gov/media/releases/2014/p0327-autism-spectrum-disorder.html

Gabig, C. S. (2011). Variability in language and reading in high-functioning autism. In Mohammad-Reza, M. (ed.), *A Comprehensive Book on Autism Spectrum Disorders*. New York: In Tech. 63–86.

Grandin, T. (2014). *The Autistic Brain: Helping Different Kinds of Minds Succeed*. Wilmington, MA: Mariner Books.

Hendricks, D. (2010). Employment and adults with autism spectrum disorders: Challenges and strategies for success. *Journal of Vocational Rehabilitation*, 32, 125–134.

Hillier, A., Campbell, H., Mastriani, K., Izzo, M. V., Kool-Tucker, A. K., Cheery, L., & Beversdorf, D. Q. (2007). Two-year evaluation of vocational support program for adults on the autism spectrum. *Career development for exceptional individuals*, 30(1), 35–47.

Kok, N. (2014, April 12). *Professor Brawn Café: The Business of Doing Good*. Retrieved from http://blog.nus.edu.sg/nm3211/2014/04/12/828/

Muller, E., Schuler, A., Burton, B. A., & Yates, G. B. (2003). Meeting the vocational support needs of individuals with Asperger Syndrome and other autism spectrum disabilities. *Journal of Vocational Rehabilitation*, 18, 163–175.

Ozonoff, S., Dawson, G., & McPartland, J. (2002). *A Parent's Guide to Asperger Syndrome and High-Functioning Autism: How to Meet the Challenges and Help Your child Thrive*. New York: Guilford Press.

Seligman, M. E. P. (2009). *Authentic Happiness*. New York: Free Press.

Seligman, M. E. P. & Csikszentmihalyi, M. (2000). Positive psychology: An introduction. *American Psychologist*, 55(1), 5–14.

Stankova, T. & Trajkovski, V. (2010). Attitudes and opinions of employers, employees, and parents about the employment of people with autism in the Republic of Macedonia. *The Journal of Special Education and Rehabilitation,* 11, 16–29.

Taylor, J. L. & Seltzer, M. M. (2011). Employment and post-secondary educational activities for young adults with autism spectrum disorders during the transition to adulthood. *Journal of Autism and Developmental Disorders,* 41, 566–574.

Wilczynski, S. M., Trammell, B., & Clarke, L. S. (2013). Improving employment outcomes among adolescents and adults on the autism spectrum. *Psychology in the Schools,* 50(9), 876–887.

Winter-Messiers, M. A. (2007). From tarantulas to toilet brushes: Understanding the special interest areas of children and youth with Asperger Syndrome. *Remedial and Special Education,* 28(3), 140–152.

Printed in the United States
By Bookmasters